Silent Strength

"Glenn Collard reminds me of Joseph as another faithful, humble man of *Silent Strength*. I commend his offering here as a deep, profound meditation from one who's given his life to service to the Lord that Joseph knew even better than we do."

—**JAMES C. HOWELL**, Senior Pastor, Myers Park United Methodist Church, Charlotte, North Carolina

"*Silent Strength* is a powerful call for men to grow in maturity and leave a legacy that lasts. Dr. Glenn Collard reminds us that true legacy is not possessions, but an investment in people, memories, values, faith, and purpose that endure for generations. Drawing on the quiet strength of St. Joseph, this is a timely, Spirit-breathed resource for any man committed to living with purpose, humility, and unwavering strength."

—**SCOTT INGEGNERI**, Executive Director, ACT International

"This book is a special and important undertaking, a unique summary of the rich meaning of maturity: the discovery of the life and spirituality of Joseph, the earthly father of Jesus of Nazareth, a quiet, faithful, and obedient man about whom we seem to know very little. It is a courageous investigation that follows in the footsteps of a mature man. In contemporary culture, we are in great need of this message. It invites us to spiritual and emotional growth, to consciously face ourselves, to surpass our own desires, and to reflect on our heritage. I trust that we will soon be able to read it in Hungarian!"

—**LÁSZLÓ A. KHALED**, District Superintendent, United Methodist Church Hungary

"Growing in maturity and leaving a legacy are essential, constitutive realities of being human, of living a meaningful life. Dr. Collard's book offers his creative reflections on manhood, following these two essential tracks, thus helping the reader in his own journey to maturity and building a meaningful legacy. A solid Christian worldview and faith, over forty years of international Christian ministry, combined with a fulfilled personal journey as husband, father, grandfather, and great-grandfather are sufficient guarantees that the reading is worthwhile."

—**Silviu E. Rogobete**, Director, Doctoral School of Philosophy, Sociology and Political Science, West University of Timisoara, Romania

Silent Strength

The Power of a Mature Man

Glenn T. Collard

Foreword by James Dana Bryan

RESOURCE *Publications* · Eugene, Oregon

SILENT STRENGTH
The Power of a Mature Man

Copyright © 2025 Glenn T. Collard. All rights reserved. Except for brief quotations in critical publications or reviews, no part of this book may be reproduced in any manner without prior written permission from the publisher. Write: Permissions, Wipf and Stock Publishers, 199 W. 8th Ave., Suite 3, Eugene, OR 97401.

Resource Publications
An Imprint of Wipf and Stock Publishers
199 W. 8th Ave., Suite 3
Eugene, OR 97401

www.wipfandstock.com

PAPERBACK ISBN: 979-8-3852-6318-9
HARDCOVER ISBN: 979-8-3852-6319-6
EBOOK ISBN: 979-8-3852-6320-2
VERSION NUMBER 11/13/25

Unless otherwise noted, Scripture quotations are taken from the (NASB®) New American Standard Bible®, copyright © 1960, 1971, 1977 by The Lockman Foundation. Used by permission. All rights reserved. lockman.org.

Scripture quotations marked ESV are from the ESV® Bible (The Holy Bible, English Standard Version®), © 2001 by Crossway, a publishing ministry of Good News Publishers. Used by permission. All rights reserved.

Scripture quotations marked (NLT) are taken from the Holy Bible, New Living Translation, copyright © 1996, 2004, 2015 by Tyndale House Foundation. Used by permission of Tyndale House Publishers, Carol Stream, Illinois 60188. All rights reserved.

Scripture quotations marked (RSV) are from the Revised Standard Version of the Bible, copyright © 1946, 1952, and 1971 National Council of the Churches of Christ in the United States of America. Used by permission. All rights reserved worldwide.

Lyrics to "Find Us Faithful" by Jon Mohr © Mystic Beard Music/ASCAP (admin. By ClearBox Rights). All rights reserved. Used by permission.

This book is lovingly dedicated to my friend and pastor, Dana Bryan. Through the years—whether serving together in his church or traveling for ministry—Dana has been a steady source of wisdom, encouragement, and laughter.

He is a man who gives freely: to his family, to his friends, and to those who need a listening ear. His mentoring and coaching have been woven into these pages, and I am deeply grateful.

Dana, this dedication is just a small way
to say, thank you for being you.

Contents

Foreword by James Dana Bryan | ix
Acknowledgments | xi

Introduction | 1
Adjectives That Describe Joseph | 7

Chapter One: The Reality of a Godly Legacy | 9
Chapter Two: A Man for All Seasons | 22
Chapter Three: Joseph Up Close and Personal | 37
Chapter Four: Essentials for Maturity | 54

In Conclusion | 69

Appendix A: Two Josephs: The Old Testament Patriarch and the New Testament St. Joseph | 71
Appendix B: If— | 76
Appendix C: A Biblical Definition of Love | 78
Appendix D: The Legacy of the Apostles | 80
About the Artist Eva Crawford | 83
Bibliography | 85

Foreword

OVER TWENTY YEARS AGO, I met my friend Glenn Collard shortly after he and his wife, Dianne, returned from years of ministry in Europe. God had used them powerfully to equip the saints, but they had also endured a grief no parent should ever face. Their story—told so beautifully in Dianne's book *I Choose to Forgive*—left a lasting impression on me. When they resettled in the United States, I saw God continue to use them in fresh and meaningful ways.

From the start, I was struck by Glenn's laser focus on his family and his future. He wasn't just raising children—he was building a legacy. The family covenant and mission statement he and Dianne crafted weren't just words on paper; they were a declaration of identity under the headship of Christ. Every member of the Collard family knew who they were and why they were here.

Two decades later, Glenn and I still meet for coffee every week. We share our hearts, our struggles, and our victories. With more years behind us than ahead, we talk often about the things that truly matter—faith, family, and finishing well. Glenn's life reminds me that maturity is not about age but about the intentional pursuit of wisdom, character, and love.

This book captures that spirit. It's not a lofty sermon or a collection of clichés. It's Glenn's life poured onto the page—a story of faith refined by suffering and shaped by hope. He invites you, the reader, to consider what kind of man you want to become and what kind of legacy you want to leave.

Foreword

If you're willing to engage, this book will challenge you to grow. It will call you to live with clarity and conviction, to love deeply, and to finish well. Glenn doesn't just write about maturity and legacy—he lives it. And I believe the truths he shares here have the power to impact generations.

I'm honored to call Glenn my friend and brother in Christ. My prayer is that this book will inspire you to live with the same focus, courage, and faith.

I commend Glenn and this book to you.

Rev. J. Dana Bryan

Acknowledgments

It would be a great injustice if I failed to salute two very godly women in my life, without whose help the finished product of this book would not have been written or published.

I refer first to my beloved wife of sixty years, Dr. Dianne B. Collard. We are not only life partners but also partners in ministry for all these sixty-plus years, with no intention of ever ceasing to serve our Lord.

The other remarkable person is my daughter, Wendy Skenderi, MA, LCMHCS, LPC-S. She is a full-time Christian counselor, my only daughter, the mother of two daughters, and now the grandmother of two granddaughters, making me a great-grandfather.

Lastly, I want to acknowledge my entire family circle: three children of my own (two sons and one daughter), one daughter-in-law, one son-in-law, five granddaughters, two grandsons-in-law, and two great-granddaughters—so far!

They have provided me with a living "lab" to practice my calling, and they continue to teach me about love, faith, and legacy.

Introduction

EVERY BOOK WRITTEN REVEALS a purpose and a passion motivating the author. In these pages, you will quickly realize that my passion is *legacy* and *maturity*. My purpose is to inspire readers to embrace these concepts in ways that can transform their lives.

Through my observations of contemporary culture, I've come to see that many men have lost their way. There is widespread confusion about what it truly means to be a man. Too often, men have surrendered their God-given uniqueness and accepted the distorted narratives our culture imposes. As a result, many drift through life, chasing a hollow version of masculinity—one rooted in machismo, control, and emotional suppression. The message they receive is clear: "man up," don't show feelings, and prove your manhood through physical strength or dominance. This misguided pursuit leaves many men disconnected from their true identity.

I believe all people leave a legacy. The real question is, is it the legacy you want to leave—the way you hope to be remembered? A godly legacy cultivates healthy, lasting relationships with family and friends as you grow older. The fruits of such a life are deeply rewarding. This book explores what it means for men to be *intentional* about leaving a godly legacy. Chapter 1 will give you a clear overview of this vision.

Silent Strength

INTRODUCING ST. JOSEPH

Researching and writing this book has been a meaningful and enjoyable journey—though it demanded a level of discipline I don't often tap into. I've learned a great deal and gained a deeper affinity for St. Joseph, whom I consider a "man for all seasons." We'll explore many of the things Scripture and other history sources reveal about him, and even more about his character, in the pages ahead.

You might wonder, why focus on Joseph, given how little is recorded about him in the New Testament? Matthew provides the most information. Luke highlights the one episode when Jesus remained in Jerusalem at twelve. John mentions him only once.

So, why study Joseph? Because he provides a compelling model of mature manhood. As men, our aim is to grow in maturity—especially in our emotional and spiritual lives. I believe Joseph offers a strong example of godly, wholehearted maturity. Maturity, after all, is the goal of living life well. And Joseph shows us how.

It's my desire to offer men a selection of insights and tools to help you embrace the challenge of growing into the man God designed you to become. As Eugene Peterson so beautifully put it, we are all on "a long obedience in the same direction."[1] The apostle Paul captured this same vision when he wrote, "We proclaim Him, admonishing every man and teaching every man with all wisdom, that we may present every man complete in Christ" (Col 1:28). Paul is clearly describing maturity.

As you read, I encourage you to reflect honestly on your own character. Where are you growing? Where do you need work? I'll present concepts to guide your self-assessment, and practical steps to help you move forward. We all need a model to follow—and Joseph is one of the best. As we go, you'll see more clearly the ingredients of growth and how they can shape a whole new way of living.

---

1. Peterson, *Long Obedience*.

Introduction

A PICTURE OF TRANSFORMATION

Picture a baseball player languishing in the minor leagues. His defensive skills are excellent—major league ready—but his offensive game is lacking. He doesn't know exactly why he's struggling until a seasoned coach watches his swing and identifies flaws he couldn't see on his own. With coaching, his perspective shifts. He sees his game in a new light. That paradigm shift becomes the turning point in his success.

This book can serve as that coach—helping you spot things you may not have noticed in yourself. It can be a tool for mentoring and discipleship, one-on-one or in groups. I hope men like you will use this resource together, forming a tribe—a band of brothers committed to growing into godly maturity.

LOOK FOR A MODEL

When my children were young, I read the Christmas story to them every Advent. Over time, I developed a deep appreciation for Joseph, the earthly father of Jesus. His quiet, faithful role in the life of Christ has fascinated me—perhaps for more reasons than the Gospel writers explicitly state.

I've spent considerable time pondering Joseph, researching him, and growing in admiration for what he can teach me as a man, a husband, and a father. My personal goal is to grow into full maturity, and I see Joseph as one of Scriptures' clearest examples of a mature man.

Think about the responsibilities Joseph carried and how faithfully he fulfilled them. Imagine being the man God chose to raise Jesus: to teach him carpentry, the Scriptures, and how to live as a man. That would challenge the best of men. And Joseph was among the best. God chose him because he was faithful to God, righteous in all his ways, obedient, patient, a servant to his wife and his God, and willing to sublimate his own desires for the sake of Mary and Jesus. These qualities are strongly implied in the Gospel of Matthew.

So, here's a question for you: when you think of nativity scenes at Christmas, where is Joseph commonly placed? If you're thinking "in the background," you are spot on. The church has long understood his quiet posture. But this isn't to downplay his importance—it's to honor his character. Joseph didn't need recognition. He found joy in his family's success. He didn't dominate; he supported. That's maturity.

Picture the nativity again. Can you see Joseph—standing off to the side, head bowed in awe, quietly absorbing the weight of his responsibility? Luke tells us Mary pondered the angel's message. I believe Joseph, too, was pondering the enormous task entrusted to them both.

Imagine fleeing Bethlehem in the dead of night to escape Herod's wrath. Joseph led Mary and Jesus through the darkness, likely uncertain of the road ahead. Surely his face revealed the tension and fear of that journey. And perhaps even the donkey understood the gravity of the moment. (Remember Num 22, when God used a donkey to speak to Balaam? If a donkey once saw what a prophet could not, maybe this one sensed something sacred, too.)

INITIATE A PLAN

When I speak of *maturity*, I also mean *character development*. We'll explore how our brains develop across five key life stages—and how we, like Joseph, are invited to confront our nature and pursue emotional and spiritual growth for a lifetime.

It's my conviction that a godly legacy is only possible for Christian men. But just *being* a Christian man doesn't make you mature—any more than living in a garage makes you a car.

My prayer is that you'll begin the long journey toward becoming the man God wants you to be. I can assure you—the work is worth it.

Sprinkled throughout this book, you'll discover how to recognize immaturity, how to pursue growth, and how to assess your progress. Along the way, I'll introduce several key concepts that define mature living. Reflect on them as you read. Ponder

Introduction

them deeply—just as Mary and Joseph pondered the weight of their calling.

KEY WORDS OF GROWTH AND MATURITY

Legacy is the principle of investing in people. Legacy can be that which is an influence of faith to any people we are in relationship with, such as family, friends, church community, and colleagues. Then future generations will be impacted by that legacy. "For God is not unjust so as to forget your work and the love which you have shown toward His name, in having ministered and still ministering to the saints" (Heb 6:10).

My people/my tribe are the ones you identify with; the ones you have faithfully associated with over many years, sharing events, sorrow and joy, walking through life together, and doing life deeply.

Community is a group that shares common values and a worldview, living in close proximity and committing to personal growth, accountability, and spiritual development together. They provide nurture, encouragement, accountability, and motivation as well as multiple role models for themselves and their children and grandchildren.

Attachment is the result of bonding which begins at conception. It is the indispensable element to an enduring relationship with a person over time. Attachment speaks of sticking together, like something glued. It's the foundation of long-term relationships.

Bonding is a process of building attachment—marked by shared joy, closeness, and a desire to be with someone meaningful.

Hesed is a rich Hebrew word often translated as loving-kindness, steadfast love, loyalty, or mercy. It's love in action.

Relationship means the result of long-term attachment, established through trust, care, and shared life over time.

Maturity is the intentional pursuit of wholeness, including emotional, behavioral, social, spiritual, and depth of character.

Joy is the state of emotional peace and rest hardwired from conception, allowing us to live as God designed.

Fear is the other hardwired emotion from conception. Our lifelong challenge is learning to manage fear so that we can live in joy.

DISCUSSION QUESTIONS AND PERSONAL REFLECTIONS RELATED TO THE INTRODUCTION

1. Why do you think having a role model is especially important for men today?

2. Has anyone ever looked to you as a role model? How did that affect you—positively or negatively?

3. What does the responsibility of being a role model mean to you? How have you handled the expectations—both your own and those of the men or younger people who look up to you?

4. As you begin this book, what do you hope to discover about yourself, your faith, or your legacy?

Adjectives That Describe Joseph

THESE ARE DESCRIPTORS OF Joseph that are wrapped in the pages of this book. You will encounter these in various ways as you read the story of this remarkable man. He truly is a man of deep character and a lodestar to attract us to emulate him.

Accountable: he was willing to answer to authority

Caring: he consistently put his family's needs ahead of his own, to ensure safety, wellness, and love

Dependable: he could be counted on; if he said yes, he would do what he committed to do

Faith: he was stalwart in his believe of, and committed to, his heavenly Father

Guardian: he took on the role of watching over his family

Humble: he was meek and lowly of heart; he did not have an exalted opinion of himself

Integrity: he was exemplary in his life to live out what he said; there was no equivocation

Just: he had a high value of morality and lived it consistently

Obedient: he did what he was told, when he was told to do it, and he had the right heart attitude

Protector: he would gladly give his life to see that his loved ones were safe

Responsible: he was put in charge of his family and could be counted on to perform his duties

Resourceful: he found ways to provide for his family when there seemed no hope

Reverent: he was instinctively responsive and respectful to everyone and especially his God

Self-Sacrificing: he gave up what he wanted, or might have wanted, to someone else; whatever it took, he was willing to give

Sublimated: he accepted the authority and/or will of someone else—of God first and then others

Teacher: he imparted information, life skills, and training to Jesus

Trusting: he was convinced of God's providence and ability to lead him

Zeal: he poured all his energy into the task he was given

DISCUSSION QUESTIONS AND PERSONAL REFLECTIONS: ADJECTIVES FOR JOSEPH'S CHARACTER

1. You haven't read much yet, but based on your current understanding and mental picture of St. Joseph, how do you see him? What words come to mind to describe him? Define those words in your own terms, without using a dictionary.

2. Compare your descriptions with what you're reading on the page. What similarities or differences do you notice? Take a moment to write them down and reflect on what stands out to you.

3. As you reflect on both your own view and the one presented in the book, what challenges or invitations do you sense for your own life as a man? Is there something about St. Joseph's example that you feel drawn to imitate or wrestle with?

Chapter One

The Reality of a Godly Legacy

The greatest legacy you can pass on to your children and grandchildren is not your money or the other material things you have accumulated in life. The greatest legacy you can pass on to them is the legacy of your character and your faith.[1]

BILLY GRAHAM

MANY DIMENSIONS TO A LEGACY

IT WOULD BE EASY to assume that *legacy* and *inheritance* are synonyms. In fact, a quick look at the dictionary might suggest just that. But from a biblical standpoint, there's a critical difference. An inheritance is something given—usually material wealth or possessions—that can be spent, squandered, or lost. Legacy is an investment in people.

The contents of a legacy are far richer: memories, values, family history, a sense of purpose—all imparted as a gift *within* someone, not merely *to* someone. This kind of legacy endures, extending across generations, touching countless lives. "For God is not unjust so as to forget your work and the love which you have

---

1. Graham, "Greatest Legacy," para. 1.

shown toward his name, in having ministered and still ministering to the saints" (Heb 6:10).

The Bible provides powerful examples of such legacy:

From Moses to Joshua

"Then Moses called for Joshua, and as all Israel watched, he said to him, 'Be strong and courageous! For you will lead people into the land that the Lord swore to their ancestors he would give them'" (Deut 31:7 NLT).

"Now Joshua, son of Nun was full of the spirit of wisdom, for Moses had laid his hands on him. So, the people of Israel obeyed him, doing just as the Lord commanded Moses" (Deut 34:9 NLT).

From Elijah to Elisha

While Elijah prayed for rain, he sent his servant to look toward the sea. Six times the servant saw nothing. The seventh time—the number of completeness in the Old Testament—the servant said, "I saw a little cloud about the size of a man's hand rising from the sea" (1 Kgs 18:4 NLT). That cloud soon brought rain.

As the story continues, God instructed Elijah to anoint Elisha as his prophetic successor. Elijah finds Elisha plowing a field, places his cloak on him, and thus empowers him to continue the prophetic ministry in Israel. Elisha requests two things: a double portion of Elijah's spirit and time to say goodbye to his parents: "'First let me go and kiss my father and mother goodbye, and then I will go with you.' Elijah replied, 'Go on back, but think about what I've done to you.'" (1 Kgs 19:20 NLT). Legacy, in these biblical accounts, was not accidental. It was deliberate.

LEGACY IN MINISTRY

Today, many churches and ministry organizations face the challenge of leadership transition. When a church planter or founder of

The Reality of a Godly Legacy

a ministry retires or resigns, succession must be carefully planned. I've gone through this process more than once in my life of ministry. This is legacy—to the glory of God.

Legacy has succession built into it. Many verses in Scripture shine a spotlight on this idea. Elijah performed eight miracles. Elisha, who received the double portion, performed sixteen. That principle applies to parenting as well. Psalm 127 tells us that children are a heritage from the Lord. When legacy is well stewarded, it often multiplies in the next generation.

We are like that small cloud seen by Elijah's servant—a humble beginning, the full impact of which will only be revealed later. Someday, from our heavenly perspective, we may witness the ripple effect of our legacy and offer it to Jesus as our sacrifice of praise.

A PERSONAL EXAMPLE

In the early 1990s, I had the privilege of working in Albania, just after the fall of Communism. There, I helped establish the country's first Bible institute to train young Christians for ministry. Years later, my own daughter—seasoned Christian counselor in the US—returned to Albania to launch a Christian counseling center. I could never have done that. But through her, God extended my calling in ways unique to her gifts. "Like arrows in the hand of a warrior, so are the children of one's youth" (Ps 127:4). Arrows go where the warrior cannot. So it is with children. Our legacy continues through them and the others we influence. You will see this principle lived out in the New Testament in the life of St. Joseph, as you continue reading.

MORE OF MY OWN STORY

You will hear me say, time and again in this book, that my calling has been to help men understand their God-given mandate to pass on a legacy of godliness—a call that applies to all men, married or single.

From the earliest days of my marriage, I felt deeply the desire to pass on the legacy of my life to future generations. I want my influence to extend to all who come after me. The day will come when no one on earth will remember me personally, but perhaps the impact of my life will still be felt through those I've influenced. How many of them will go on to raise children of their own? How many will embrace the call to live as mature men? This is not something most people reflect on, but my appeal is simple: become aware. *Take it seriously.*

In December 1990, Dianne and I, with our youngest son Greg, left California for Vienna, Austria. Our two oldest children, Tim and Wendy, were in college and remained behind. This began for us a residence in Austria, Hungary, and Germany of fourteen years.

Austria was like a dream—picturesque mountains, charming villages, rich history, and the famed Viennese coffee culture (*café und kuchen*!). It didn't take long for me to begin thinking about the Habsburg Empire. One royal family, one dynasty, lasted 636 years and ruled over what is now Austria, Hungary, parts of the Czech Republic, Slovakia, Poland, Ukraine, Romania, Serbia, Bosnia, Slovenia, Croatia, Italy, and Germany. I wondered—how could this be? And more personally, could I establish a family that would endure?

It fit perfectly with my vision of legacy. I began to imagine a generational line of Christ-followers who would serve others, promote righteousness, and live by the words of Micah: "To do justice, to love kindness, and to walk humbly with your God" (Mic 6:8).

To that end, Dianne and I, with our adult children and spouses, created what we call a "Collard Family Covenant." Each family of our tree has a copy displayed somewhere in their home.

THE COLLARD FAMILY COVENANT

> We covenant together to live our lives in pursuit of God, serving our local churches, our community and the world. We will develop the whole person and celebrate our uniqueness while practicing forgiveness in an atmosphere of grace.

The Reality of a Godly Legacy

This covenant reflects both internal and external commitments. It speaks to values like character development and principled behavior, all flowing from our Christian commitment to live godly lives. Psalm 78 has profoundly shaped my thinking:

> I will open my mouth in a parable; I will utter dark sayings from of old, things that we have heard and known, that our fathers have told us. We will not hide them from their children, but tell to the coming generation the glorious deeds of the Lord and his might and the wonders he has done. He established a testimony in Jacob, and appointed a law in Israel, which he commanded our fathers to teach to their children, that the next generation might know them, the children yet unborn, and arise and tell them to their children, so that they should set their hope in God and not forget the work of God but keep his commandments. (Ps 78:2–7 ESV)

These verses capture the heart of biblical legacy. As parents, we are both responsible and accountable. First, to live it ourselves. Then, to pass it down to our children, grandchildren and great grandchildren—if the Lord grants us the years to see it.

A wonderful gift from my daughter was given to me for Christmas. She is a grandmother now who reflects on her life under her father, with a view and intention to do it again for her family. I can only bow in humility and gratitude for what God has produced in our lives. Thanks be to God.

CHRISTMAS POEM

Each year for Christmas I try to write at least one . . .
A bit of prose for a beloved, to increase the fun.
Typically, the theme is whimsical and cute,
A suggestive hint to guess the contents of one's loot.
But this year for Christmas I've altered my aim.
I craft a poem for reasons not the same.
Instead, my desire is to find a way to honor . . .
A collection of words strung together to ponder.

Silent Strength

I'd like to be poignant and to draw attention near
To the legacy and life of our Opa and Mimi so dear.
For it is not every family that has been given the chance
AND it's not a coincidence as can seem at first glance.
No, this legacy was meaningfully and intentionally crafted
From early commitments and mission statements drafted,
Whose principles and values were followed with care,
With integrity, with purpose, determination and prayer.
With this rhyme and the gift, I attempt to give thanks
For the present you have given, which far above purchased gifts ranks.
For I increasingly realize and am becoming aware
That the legacy you've given is quite precious and rare.
It's a rooted foundation of lives lived for Christ,
Lived well all along, for it could not be done twice.
A legacy is formed from beginning to end.
There's no chance to interrupt and start over again.
From you we see a consistent and honorable striving,
(The kind of stuff on which WE are now thriving.)
You are loving and gracious, gentle and kind,
Attentive, supportive, principled, refined.
The legacy you've woven has everything to do
With the fruit of the Spirit that's grown richly in you.
I hope someday that I can pass on the same
To my children and grandchildren, these values as named.
The best way to honor you and this legacy you've given
Is to honor the One Who from death to life has risen.
But isn't that the point of the example you've set?
Isn't that the message you've prayed your family would get?
I thank you from every fiber of my being
For giving to me a life filled with such meaning.
I offer my praise to the Father above
For allowing me to receive your "legacy of love."
With love to Opa and Mimi
On Christmas Day 2023

The Reality of a Godly Legacy

HOW THE TRANSFER OF LEGACY WORKS

My point can be illustrated effectively in the popular story of King Arthur, made into a musical called *Camelot*. In medieval England, Arthur rises from humble beginnings to become king. He brings to his reign a deep-seated desire for righteousness to rule the kingdom. Laws governing the behavior of the knights as well as the people are set up to create fairness and an orderly society. Respect of each person is a high value. Ruling is approached more as a committee by the twelve knights along with Arthur. War is forbidden. No more of the dystopian fiefdom or of a narcissistic king. All is well for a while, until power and control manifest themselves resulting in a war, destroying the utopian dream.

We pick up the story at the last scene, after the knights have gone to battle and Arthur stands alone lamenting all he thinks he has lost. And that would be true were it not for young Tom, whom Arthur discovers in the background.

From the shadows emerges the twelve-year-old boy. Arthur and Tom begin a conversation. When asked by Arthur how he knows of the knights and the kingdom rule and order of Camelot, Tom replies that he knows because of the stories people tell. Then Arthur admonishes young Tom, whom he has just knighted, to go home, to never engage in war as he has just witnessed. He further amplifies his point by instructing him to enjoy life and grow old. The point is made that history will record and people will remember.

Our lives will be remembered: through the stories people tell and the lives they live, just like Tom, who experienced the dream and will carry the possibility of extending it far into the future.

The salient points of the fictional story of King Arthur highlight the importance of a personal legacy. These are the ingredients of a legacy—a life lived well; intentionally taught; subliminally caught; remembered and rehearsed orally; and transmitted and recast in writing for future generations.

Legacy is a clear biblical concept. These are the instructions God gave Moses for his people:

Silent Strength

> And these words that I command you today shall be on your heart. You shall teach them diligently to your children, and shall talk of them when you sit in your house, and when you walk by the way, and when you lie down and when you rise up. You shall bind them as a sign on your hand, and they shall be as frontlets between your eyes. You shall write them on the doorposts of your house and on your gates. (Deut 6:6–10 ESV)

A life lived well, and transmitted and recast in writing for future generations will look like these lines of Old Testament poetry:

> But you have made me as strong as a wild ox. You have anointed me with the finest oil. My eyes have seen the downfall of my enemies: my ears have heard the defeat of my wicked opponents. But the godly will flourish like palm trees and grow strong like the cedars of Lebanon. For they are transplanted to the Lord's house. They flourish in the courts of our God. Even in old age they will still produce fruit; they will remain vital and green. They will declare, "The Lord is just! He is my rock! There is no evil in him!" (Ps 92:10–15 NLT)

Dianne and I are tremendously grateful for our adult children who have embraced and live out our family covenant. They have embodied the need for an intentional legacy for their own kids. We now have two great-grandchildren. And should the Lord allow, I'll live long enough to see them take their place in the Collard dynasty of people living well, loving and serving the Lord, and passing on the heritage to their children also. So that's four generations and counting. How many more will it take to out-live the Habsburgs? I will observe that from my mansion in glory.

The Reality of a Godly Legacy

TWO STORIES OF LEGACY

Story One

You may never have heard of Edward Kimball. He's not a household name, but God used him to create a legacy that ultimately impacted someone you *do* know.

Kimball was a faithful Sunday school teacher of teenage boys. One of them, a seventeen-year-old working in a shoe store, wasn't initially interested in spiritual things—but Kimball took an interest in him anyway. That teenager's name? Dwight L. Moody.

Moody went on to become an evangelist with an astounding reach to one hundred million people. He also founded Moody Bible Institute and Moody Church in Chicago. But that's just the beginning. From Moody's ministry came a stream of leaders and theologians:

- F. B. Meyer, a British pastor, influenced
- J. Wilbur Chapman, who then impacted
- Billy Sunday, a major evangelist in the early twentieth century.
- Billy Sunday influenced Mordecai Ham, who eventually preached to a young man you *do* know—Billy Graham.[2]

We cannot know what God will do through a life lived well and a legacy intentionally built.

Story Two

While living in Germany, I had the pleasure of attending the internationally known *Passion Play* in Oberammergau, Bavaria. This is a week-long reenactment of the final days of Christ's life—his crucifixion, death, and resurrection.

The story goes that in 1634, a plague was ravaging the surrounding region. In desperation, the townspeople of Oberammergau prayed, asking God to spare them. He did. In gratitude, they

2. Priestap, "It Started."

vowed to reenact the passion of Christ once every ten years. That vow has now been kept for nearly four hundred years. The entire town participates. People leave their jobs to act, sing, and serve in a massive outdoor production. Costumes are period accurate, the staging is elaborate, and live animals help bring the biblical scenes to life.

What astonishes me is this: those villagers made a commitment not just for themselves, but for their descendants—for generations to come. They trusted that their children and grandchildren would carry on the work. *That's legacy*. Imagine making a commitment today that your family would still be honoring four hundred years later.

I stand in awe of the power of legacy. Only God knows what he will do with what we build. We don't commit to a legacy hoping for fame or long-lasting influence. We commit because *God calls us to commit*. He calls us to leave footprints—evidence that we were here and that we followed him.

Legacy contributes to God's great work of restoring his creation and drawing people to himself. If all the lives influenced by godly legacies could be lined up around the world, the train would stretch for myriads—numbers beyond counting. What God does with it is part of his sovereignty. To him be the glory.

RECOGNIZE AND COMMIT TO YOUR OWN LEGACY

The raison d'être—the reason for being—is to recognize that every person leaves a legacy. When you pass into eternity, you leave behind who you were, what you stood for, and what you contributed to the lives of those within your sphere of influence. Everyone leaves a legacy—whether by design or by default. So, ask yourself, "Am I working on the legacy I want to leave?" To leave a legacy that is strong, unequivocally centered on family, and committed to the glory of God requires a *fully mature man*. That includes *every man*—married or single, father or not. Every man has influence, and every relationship is an opportunity to leave a mark that honors God. The objective is to grow into what Paul describes: "That

The Reality of a Godly Legacy

we may present every man complete in Christ" (Col 1:28). And here are the unspoken—and often avoided—questions behind all this: "Am I dealing with the issues in my life that reveal holes in my character?" "Have I simply learned to mask my immaturity?" "Am I willing to face those weak areas and begin the hard work of growth"? The goal of legacy assumes we're working on our character—because *developing a godly legacy requires a mature man*.

I propose that St. Joseph is a model of a mature man for us to emulate. As you read my reasons why, my hope is that you will feel something stir in your spirit—a challenge to recognize and address the areas in your life that point to immaturity; those hidden character flaws will hold you back. They will crowd out any attempts you make to focus on your legacy. This will take courage.

In the appendix and bibliography, I've included resources to help you begin or continue that personal project of growth and legacy.

I close this section on legacy with the lyrics of a song written by Jon Mohr and performed by Steve Green on his album *People Need the Lord*. I first heard this song during the early days of my grief recovery from the loss of my son. Its words spoke deeply to my hurting heart, prompting me to reflect on my call to missions in Europe and my longing to leave a lasting legacy—both within my family and through my ministry. Through this song, I found renewed hope for my future and a deeper awareness of God's hand upon my life.

These lyrics beautifully capture the heart of a godly legacy, reminding us that the lives we touch and the love we share echo into eternity.

FIND US FAITHFUL

> We're pilgrims on the journey
> Of the narrow road,
> And those who've gone before us
> Line the way.
> Cheering on the faithful,

Silent Strength

Encouraging the weary,
Their lives a stirring testament
To god's sustaining grace.

Chorus
O may all who come behind us
Find us faithful,
May the fire of our devotion
Light their way.
May the footprints that we leave,
Lead them to believe,
And the lives we live
Inspire them to obey.
O may all who come behind us
Find us faithful.

Surrounded by so great
A cloud of witnesses,
Let us run the race
Not only for the prize,
But as those who've gone before us.
Let us leave to those behind us,
The heritage of faithfulness
Passed on thru godly lives.

Chorus

After all our hopes and dreams
Have come and gone,
And our children sift thru all
We've left behind,
May the clues that they discover,
And the mem'ries they uncover,
Become the light that leads them,
To the road we each must find.

Oh, may all who come behind us,
Find us faithful.[3]

---

3. Mohr, "Find Us Faithful."

DISCUSSION QUESTIONS AND PERSONAL REFLECTIONS: THE REALITY OF A GODLY LEGACY

1. When Elijah told Elisha, "Go back, but think about what I've done to you," imagine what Elisha was thinking. He likely began the day working in the field, completely unaware of the sudden visit from Elijah. He was probably caught off guard. How would you respond if something like this interrupted your daily life?

2. When St. Joseph received God's call through the message of an angel, how do you think he felt? What might have been going through his mind?

3. Do you see receiving a legacy like this—as Elisha and Joseph did—as a privilege or a burden? Why? In what ways?

4. What role does love play in building or passing on a legacy? (You'll read about hesed love in chapter 4.)

5. What's your plan for growing your own legacy—personally, spiritually, and relationally?

Chapter Two

A Man for All Seasons

IN THE VOLUME OF these pages, I invite you to trek with me to understand St. Joseph, earthly father of Jesus. By understanding better, you may find motivation to seek him as a role model. May you be inspired to adopt for yourself his love for God and people, and his self-sacrificing service for God. Church father Gregory of Nazianzen in the fourth century said, "The Almighty has concentrated in St. Joseph, as in a sun of unrivaled luster, the combined light and splendor of all the other saints."[1]

This quote attests to a plethora of saints in the past who understood Joseph in the same light—of irreproachable character, and a man of *silence and strength*. For me, he has become a model of what it means to be fully mature in every area of life. I have learned much from him. There is much he can teach all of us. Follow me as I guide you through the major elements of this amazing man's life.

WHAT'S IN A NAME?

"Joseph also includes meanings such as 'to increase,' 'to grow,' or 'to repeat.'"[2] How appropriate for the role God asked him to play!

---

1. Quoted in Calloway, *Consecration to St. Joseph*, 86.
2. Walshe, *Saint Joseph*, 36.

God tasked him with the care of Mary and Jesus. His willingness to participate in God's plan allowed him to become the model of a mature man for the world's Christians for nearly two thousand years. In echoes of Abraham, God said, "Look toward heaven, and number the stars, if you are able to number them" (Gen 15:5 ESV). God made him the increaser.

WHO IS THIS MAN?

Clearly, Joseph was not the biological father of Jesus. Still, he cooperated with God to do what no man before or after has been asked to do. He was willing to participate in the incarnation, ultimately leading to God's offer of redemption demonstrated in the crucifixion and resurrection. Yet he never witnessed those events—certainly not from earth's vantage point. He saw his work in "fathering" the Messiah come to fruition from the heavenly realms. When Jesus became incarnate, in his humanness he required the same care as we do—love, food, education, shelter, clothing, and protection, for example. His divine nature needed no human care. Regarding his human nature, Jesus put himself under the laws of human growth and development. He needed the masculinity of a father to imitate. He learned this from Joseph the carpenter. And what about manners and customs of his culture? He learned those also from his father. Though Joseph was not Jesus's father by generation, he was his father in upbringing, care, and the affection of his heart.

Joseph knew the Old Testament well. He assiduously lived up to the teachings and commands of Moses:

> Hear O Israel: The Lord our God, the Lord is one. You shall love the Lord your God with all your heart and with all your soul and with all your might. And these words that I command you today shall be on your heart. You shall teach them diligently to your children, and shall talk of them when you sit in your house, and when you walk by the way, and when you lie down, and when you rise. You shall bind them as a sign upon your hand, and

they shall be as frontlets between your eyes. You shall write them on the doorposts of your house and on your gates. (Deut 6:4–8 ESV)

This, and much more, was Joseph's role as Jesus's earthly father. He performed all his fatherly duties well. We will see this unfold in the pages to follow.

A REVERENT MAN

Many early church fathers recognized Joseph as a reverent man, in awe at the child Mary carried, yet considering himself unworthy to be her husband. Matthew aligns Joseph as a descendent of royalty, a son of David, in Matt 1:20. The visitation of the angel confirmed Joseph's role as the earthly father, appealing to his sense of belonging in the line of God's promises through David. Both Matthew and Luke affirm Joseph as the son of David.

The angel brought affirmation to Joseph. Another early church father, Peter Chrysologus, in the fifth century wrote,

> Joseph, son of David, do not be afraid. What you see in her is virtue, not sin. This is not a human fall, but a divine descent. Here is a reward, not guilt. This is an engagement from heaven, not a detriment to the body. This is the victory of a person; it is the secret of the Judge. Here is the victory of him who knows the case, not the penalty of torture. Here is not man's stealthy deed, but the treasure of God. Here is not the cause of death, but of life.[3]

Two important characteristics stand out in Matt 1:20: responsibility and obedience. Joseph's response to the angel and his consideration of his role exemplify these traits. More on this to come.

HIS OPTIONS TO CHOOSE

How do you suppose you would respond if an angel made a personal appearance to you? If you were in the room with Joseph,

---

3. Quoted in Calloway, *Consecration to St. Joseph*, 140.

what advice would you give him? Bible scholars reduce his choices to three perspectives:

1. Suspicion perspective—he could decide to divorce Mary and, under the law, have her stoned. Even then, such occasions seldom happened.

2. Stupefaction perspective—he was stupefied by her pregnancy, he was unable to think clearly. He didn't doubt her innocence, but was confused, so he might divorce her.

3. Reverence perspective—he didn't doubt her innocence but doubted his own worthiness to live with her. He was willing to remove himself to protect her mystery.

The Greek word for divorce is *apoluo*, which depending on context can mean separate, conceal, hide, distance from oneself, or divorce.[4] Most translations use "divorce." I prefer to think of Joseph as self-effacing. It fits his character better than a punitive response or living out the letter of the law. He had a numinous call from God to father the God-man. "If St. Joseph passed the test by a loving willingness to sacrifice himself completely, God would bless him in a manner greater than he had blessed any other man who has ever lived."[5]

COMMUNICATION BETWEEN JOSEPH AND MARY

It's intriguing to ponder what conversations Mary and Joseph must have had. Likely Mary told Matthew about them since Matthew would probably not have known Joseph. Joseph would not have known what was going on in Mary's womb. He had no sense of hypostatic union—the combining of deity and humanity simultaneously—or incarnation. He accepted in faith what God was doing and his place as the earthly protector and overseer. He didn't doubt Mary; he doubted himself.

---

4. Calloway, *Consecration to St. Joseph*, 143.
5. Calloway, *Consecration to St. Joseph*, 147.

Silent Strength

With the exception of Jesus Christ, there has never been a man so selfless and heroic in love, faith, justice, reverence and humility as St. Joseph. God let Joseph know that he needed to rely on St. Joseph's willingness to always do the will of God. Jesus himself would need to rely on the humility and sacrificial love of St. Joseph in order to accomplish his saving mission. There would come a time when St. Joseph would be removed from the picture so that Jesus could teach about his Heavenly Father, but that time was not yet. Yet St. Joseph had proven himself to be a man who was reliable and obedient in the face of all sorts of events, whether advantageous or adverse. God could trust him.[6]

A PANORAMIC VIEW OF HISTORY

There is more to the story of Joseph. What about his family history, his ancestors, his education, his daily life in the village of Nazareth? Who was this mysterious person God chose?

To understand this better, it's worth getting a panoramic view of the history of the breakup of the Davidic dynasty after Solomon dies.

The kingdom broke up, with the north conquered by the Assyrians and the south by the Babylonians. Ten tribes in the north remained under the name Israel, while two tribes were united in the south under the name Judah. Our Joseph descended from Judah.

First, Israel was taken captive by the Assyrians in 727 BC. By 597 BC, the southern tribes were taken into captivity by the Babylonian empire. In 538 BC, the Persians, who had conquered the Babylonians, allowed the Jews to return to their homeland.

Then followed the Greeks who conquered the Persians, then the Romans who conquered the Greeks and converted the Jews to Roman culture. That caused the rise of the Hasmonean dynasty—led by Judah Maccabee—a Jewish priestly family who led a

---

6. Calloway, *Consecration to St. Joseph*, 151.

rebellion against the Seleucids who came to power after the break-up of the Greek Empire ruled by Alexander.

Generations later, in the second century BC, the Maccabee family of Jewish warriors led a revolution against Rome. It was the call of the Hasmoneans to Jews living in Babylon, who had lived there for many years, to return to Israel. They were able to cast out the foreign rulers in Judah and lead fellow Jews back to the laws of Moses and rule the land. They began a call to the diaspora Jews living in Babylon to return to Judah. It was about the year 100 BC. Decades later, families who responded to the call to return settled in the lower Galilee where they established two settlements. The New Testament showcases the Roman Empire's rule of Palestine at this time.

This migration of the people of the house of David in these two villages of 120 and 150 inhabitants included the family of Jacob, Joseph's family. They knew the prophecies of the Old Testament, and were greatly aware of the Messiah coming from there. As Matthew tells it, the royal line in which Joseph was born was included among the prophecies.

HIS BIRTH PLACE

This is a tale of two cities—well, hardly cities, more like villages. One named Kochba, meaning "village of the star," referring to the prophecy of Balaam: "A star shall come forth out of Jacob" (Num 24:17). Nazareth was the other town, named from Isa 11:1: "There shall come forth a shoot from the stump of Jesse," David's royal line.

The questions of where and when Joseph was born and died are a major challenge to nail down. Matthew and Luke give us clues, but indefinite clues. A simple search of the internet will suggest he was born around 30 BC. That could be true, or close—we just don't know for sure. But like other imponderables in his life, we must satisfy ourselves to wait till we get to heaven to know.

Because of his nearest ancestors' immigration from Babylonia to Palestine, I take the view of his family's immigration to settle in the village of Nazareth as the place of his birth.

Luke 2 tells us the journey of Joseph and Mary to Bethlehem was when Quirinius ruled, when Rome called for a census. The purpose of the census was to register the population for taxes, and to register any property such as land or houses. Of course, taxation was the primary reason.

After the glory days of David and Solomon, the Babylonians conquered Judah, deporting thousands. The house of David had lived in exile in Babylon for many generations. The Jews of this diaspora kept meticulous genealogical records of the clans of David. This was the hope they held—that someday the house would be restored. "The Lord said, 'I made a covenant with David, my chosen servant. I have sworn this oath to him: I will establish your descendants as kings forever; they will sit on your throne from now to eternity'" (Ps 89:3–4 NLT).

"They were as certain of that moment as they were of any other. It was not a speculative question *if*, but a burning question of *when*."[7] The families kept vigil, watching for the Messiah.

Matthew 1–2 places Joseph and Mary in Bethlehem. With the background we've uncovered we can see why Matthew sets the first scene of the Christmas drama in Bethlehem. Bethlehem was the seat of David's royalty. Joseph, being of the lineage of David, was obliged to make the trip. Some speculate he may even have owned property there. Mary—being great with child and ready to deliver—and Joseph were forced to make the ninety-three-mile trek to Bethlehem. Thus, they made their way to register for the census.

JOSEPH'S EDUCATION

It was in the years of Babylonian captivity, leading into the four hundred years between the writings of the Old and New Testaments, that the synagogues came into being. The synagogues became the primary source of learning for children from about four years to twelve years of age.

---

7. Aquilina, *St. Joseph and His World*, 9–10.

A Man for All Seasons

To understand this long period, it may be helpful to grasp a simple overview of the major characteristics of Jewish education during the five centuries leading to Christ:

> Fifth century BC: The written law of Moses was emphasized as foundational to learning.
>
> Fourth century BC: Aramaic was the everyday spoken language, while Hebrew remained the written language of religion.
>
> Third century BC: Under the Greek language, there was great cultural emphasis, as well as emphasis on moral values, social teachings, and the wisdom literature of Job, Proverbs, and Ecclesiastes.
>
> Second century BC: Jewish nationalism developed and education turned again to the Mosaic law.
>
> First century BC: Elementary schools are established outside the synagogue to teach reading, writing, and arithmetic to children.

The importance of a child starting school may be seen in this picture of family ceremonies. On the first day of school, the child was awakened before dawn, bathed, and dressed in a gown with fringe on it. At dawn, he was taken to the synagogue by his father and sat down at the reading desk with a scroll open to Exodus 20:2–26.

The passage was then read aloud to him, whereupon he was taken to his teacher and welcomed with open arms. He was given a slate with the alphabet and two texts of the Mosaic law. The teacher would read them as the child repeated. Following the reading, the slate was smeared with honey, while the lad was required to lick it off—symbolic of Ezekiel eating the scroll. Finally, he was given sweet cakes with passages of Scripture to eat, followed by a closing prayer. Clearly, the importance the family placed on education, regardless of when the family lived, is illustrated here. Joseph would have been schooled in this manner. No doubt Jesus was as well.

IMPONDERABLES

Here is an age-old question: Was Joseph young or old when he received the message of the birth from the angel? Who among us has never pondered it and wondered why God didn't tell us? For that matter, how old was Mary when Luke records an angel appearing to her? Unfortunately, neither of the Gospel writers explain. But the putative perspective of the historic church agrees that Mary was a mid-teenager.

Matthew didn't tell us how old Joseph was when the angel delivered the news to him of the coming birth. We are curious, of course. He was either a little older or a lot older, as in very old. The Orthodox Church maintains he was actually "quite elderly." In the Catholic Church, some say older and some younger.

Of all the ways Joseph has been seen over the centuries, with titles given him by the traditional church such as protector, guardian, model, or workman, he would have had to be younger to live up to such nomenclature. As Mother Angelica once quipped, "Old Men don't walk to Egypt"[8]—a journey of at least forty miles to the border. And we know they continued the journey to pierce the heart of the desert in Egypt and dwell there, waiting for the news to return. As they remained in Egypt, they very likely identified with the Jews who were prominent in Egypt at that time.

THE REST OF THE STORY

So, back to our story from Bethlehem to Egypt. After Mary's forty days of purification and Jesus's circumcision, the angel appeared for the second time, awakened Joseph, and warned him to take Mary and Jesus to Egypt. The message was imperative. They grabbed what they could, and with Mary on a donkey holding Jesus while Joseph took the reins, they headed down the road.

---

8. Quoted in Calloway, *Consecration to St. Joseph*, 113.

A Man for All Seasons

TWO POSSIBLE MODES OF TRANSPORT

Our holy family must have been harried and hassled. We don't know which mode of transport they took. We assume they traveled by donkey with Joseph walking alongside. Their route was a common trade route trafficked by people for centuries. Their journey took them west to the Mediterranean coast, then southward for one hundred miles along the coast, to Gaza. From Gaza to the country of the Nabateans, a nomadic tribe who had spread across the southern Arabian Peninsula. The holy family must have breathed a little easier in that area, because the Nabatean rulers were quarreling with Herod at that time, resisting his overtures to annex them. Up to this point, they had traveled by night and hidden themselves during the day, so as not to be found by Herod's spies.

The miles piled up as they made their way forward to Alexandria. To that point it would have been over three hundred miles total. A donkey could travel about twelve to fifteen miles per day, depending on the road conditions and stops to rest along the way. It would have taken them about a month thus far.

But they could have traveled from the port at Jaffa by boat to Alexandria, a journey of over two hundred miles. If the sailboat could go a speed of eight miles an hour the journey would have taken about two days.

I'm still assuming, and will assume for the duration of this story, they traveled by land. So, finally, they made their way into Egypt, passing through the territory of the Nabateans, presumably somewhere near the eastern part of the Nile delta. We know from history there were synagogues and enclaves of Jews existing in Nabatea and Egypt. Likely our family found help and assistance in different ways as they traveled. Estimates for that time are believed to be around four percent of the population in Egypt were Jews.

I quote author Mike Aquilina: "Jews served at the Egyptian royal court and in the high ranks of the military. In this land where they had once been enslaved, they were now enjoying a revival in literary culture. The city of Alexandria had a large Jewish population that occupied two sizable neighborhoods by the seashore.

Silent Strength

There were even suburbs and distant exurbs known as 'villages of the Jews.'"[9] Our Coptic brothers and sisters tell us our holy family lodged for a time in twenty-six different locations, from Alexandria on the Mediterranean to Assiut in the south.

One of Joseph's character traits was his resourcefulness. There is assumption by some historians that Joseph would have known some Jewish families who lived in the eastern part of Egypt, who could have helped the holy family along the way. Plus, Joseph being a skilled laborer, he could do odd jobs, handyman jobs, to provide for his family's needs.

Pause for a moment to ponder these questions: "How did Joseph finance the journey?" "I wonder if it wasn't the gold, frankincense, and myrrh?" "Did Jehovah-Jireh, the Lord who directed all this, provide by sending the wise men from the east with what they would need?" "Did the same donkey carrying Mary and Jesus, last the whole time and be the vehicle to return them?"

In spite of infrequent localized conflicts with Egyptians, Joseph and his family could live somewhat normally, safely out of the grip of Herod, where they could raise their son in the traditions of their ancestors. Joseph could work and ply his skills. As a *tekton* he was skilled as a craftsman in wood, metal, and stone for building. It probably would have been fairly easy to stay employed due to the economy of Egypt then. He probably even learned, to some degree, the Greek language. In fact, it was probably in Egypt where Jesus first observed his father plying his trade.

What else they did while in Egypt is a very interesting aspect to think about. We know from records in the Coptic Eastern Orthodox Church the family visited many different sites down the river Nile, as far as Assiut in upper Egypt. This was a distance of seventy-five miles. They must have been in Assiut when an angel appeared to him for the *third* time. Joseph received the message: "OK, the coast is clear. Herod is no more. You can go home!" This news had to have given an exciting sense of relief, only to have their joy diminished by the dread of the return travel. The roads were rocky, filled with holes, and perilous with bandits and various

---

9. Aquilina, *St. Joseph and His World*, 84.

miscreants. No fast food and no hotels. I wonder what Joseph first thought. As the provider, I think it's logical that he was concerned about things such as safety, supplies for food and water, normal hygiene, and the like.

There were other stressors that must have been part of the conversation between Mary and Joseph for the whole trip. They no doubt heard Herod's kingdom was divided by Caesar Augustus between Herod's children. I can imagine the anxiety that must have grown the closer they came to Jerusalem. Joseph made the decision where they would land, after his *third visit* from an angel, Matt 2:22. After weighing the consequences as to which leader would be best, his decision was to stay out of the Jerusalem area. He chose to return to Galilee where he had family who were part of the great return of his extended family, and many, many others who came out of Babylon from years before.

They pulled up stakes in Assiut (where today there still is an ancient Coptic monastery dedicated to Mary), and launched themselves toward Palestine and home.

The burning question now is, "How long were they in Egypt?" Sadly, this is another unanswerable question. The traditional view is their time in Egypt would have been four years. The Coptic Orthodox Church can identify twenty-six different locations. This claim by our brothers and sisters in the Coptic Church is based on tradition. But we do know their departure would have been after Herod died, and he died in April of the year 4 BC. The duration of their stay in Egypt, therefore, would have been from sometime after the Magi left Jerusalem to sometime after Herod's death. We know that Joseph knew when Herod died because the angel told him in his *third dream*.

DID JESUS HAVE SIBLINGS

A natural question that arises in exploring the family of Jesus is, "Did Jesus have siblings?" Protestants honor Joseph and Mary yet generally accept that they likely had other children. The Catholic Church, supported by many church fathers and mothers, maintains that the

Greek word traditionally translated as "brothers" and "sisters" actually means "cousins." This is a reasonable linguistic argument.

I pause here to note that in believing James and Jude—authors of the epistles bearing their names—were half-brothers of Jesus sheds light on the earthly family of Joseph and Mary. James, the leader of the Jerusalem church, was recognized as the Lord's brother by fathers of the early church like Origen (AD 185–253), Eusebius (AD 265–340), and Jerome (AD 340–420). Jude likewise refers to himself as the brother of James (Jude 1:1), and Paul called James "the Lord's brother" (Gal 1:19). This difference in interpretation between Protestant and Catholic traditions remains one on which we must agree to disagree.

Why does this matter to the story of Joseph? Because understanding the elements of normal family life in Jesus's time helps us imagine the household into which he was born and grew up. Jesus would have had natural interactions with siblings. It's even reasonable to speculate that Jude and Jesus might have experienced mild conflicts or differences of opinion, especially since Jude reportedly did not believe Jesus was the Messiah until after the resurrection.

However, the Catholics have not always agreed within their own ranks. In my research I found the following story very interesting: "In the fourth century, a bishop named Bonoso from Illyricum (that is, modern day areas of Albania, Montenegro, Croatia) was rebuked by his brother bishops and stripped of his episcopacy for teaching that Mary and Joseph had more children after Jesus was born. The pope at the time, St. Pope Siricius, wrote a letter to the faithful bishops in Illyricum, thanking them for disciplining the errant bishop."[10] Some of us do not agree, but as I said, there is no reason to separate over the issue.

Some speculate if Joseph was older, those other children might have been from a previous marriage, with a wife who had died before Joseph was betrothed to Mary. The Orthodox Church holds this view.

The Catholic Church is committed to the theology that both Mary and Joseph were perpetually virgins, affirming that those

---

10. Calloway, *Consecration to St. Joseph*, 127.

other children were cousins of Jesus. Further, the Catholic Church believes the submission by Mary to the angel's message was to remain pure for a life time. And Mary said, "Behold, I am the servant of the Lord: let it be to me according to your word" (Luke 1:38 ESV). Protestants, by contrast, have no theological angst accepting Mary and Joseph had other children.

Having other children after the virgin birth does not undermine the doctrine of the virgin birth nor affect the significance of salvation. Similarly, while Joseph's exact age remains uncertain, the logic and reasonableness of a younger Joseph is compelling, and many prefer that view. This helps us picture natural family life—parents, children, relationships—into which Jesus was born.

In chapter 3, we will explore the life of the holy family more closely. Every family has a family system—the dynamics, interactions, and shared beliefs that shape how family members relate to one another and the outside world. Children are socialized both formally and informally, observing and adopting behaviors, values, and norms. This exchange within the family system solidifies the identity of each member as well as the family unit itself.

DISCUSSION QUESTIONS AND PERSONAL REFLECTIONS: A MAN FOR ALL SEASONS

1. Even today, people often name their children with specific meaning—sometimes to honor a family tradition. Do you know if your name was chosen for a special reason or purpose by your parents? How does that affect how you see yourself?

2. Read Deut 6:4–8. What does this passage mean to you personally? How do you live it out—or struggle to?

3. Why do you think it matters that so many early church fathers and mothers placed deep importance on St. Joseph? What does that say to us today?

4. Reflect on the circumstances surrounding Joseph and Mary's planned marriage—how dramatically their lives and purpose

were altered. How does that make you feel? Can you relate in any way?

5. What aspects of Israel's history pique your curiosity or invite deeper reflection?

6. What do you sometimes wish God had explained more clearly about the lives of Joseph and Mary?

7. The Catholic and Orthodox Churches teach that Mary and Joseph had no other children, while many Protestants believe they did. Does this difference matter to you? Why or why not?

8. How would you describe your own family system to someone else? What words would you use to characterize your family overall—past and present?

Chapter Three

Joseph Up Close and Personal

Having come this far in grasping Joseph's general character, background, and early actions as reported by Matthew and other historical sources, it's time to delve deeper into Joseph himself and his four dreams. First, let's consider more on the holy family in order to clearly see the family system from which Jesus came.

A LOOK INSIDE THE FAMILY

In a somewhat convincing article by Bishop Fulton J. Sheen, "Joseph was probably a young man, strong, virile, athletic, handsome, chaste, and disciplined. . . . He was not in the evening of life, but in its morning, bubbling over with energy, strength and controlled passion. . . . How much more beautiful Mary and Joseph become when we see in their lives what might be called the first Divine Romance!"[1]

Donald Calloway observes,

> The formative years of Jesus Christ were lovingly ruled by a strong young father named Joseph. It was this hardworking, caring and virtuous father who laid the foundations for the human growth and development of Jesus Christ. While there is no doubt that an old man is just as

---

1. Quoted in Calloway, *Consecration to St. Joseph*, 115–16.

capable of being holy as any young man, it takes a strong young father to teach a boy how to swing an axe, work with wood, carry lumber, walk great distances and earn a living by the sweat of his brow.[2]

These are assumptions about the relationship of Joseph and Mary and for Jesus in his formative years, but not unreasonable. My thesis is that Joseph was a mature man—one who gave full respect and sensitivity to Mary, his wife, as the chosen one of God to bring forth the God-man. Joseph would have given his all to fulfill his God-given task. To call their marriage and family a "Divine Romance" might be a little overimaginative, but the romantic in me wants to believe it was lived out that way.

JOSEPH AND MARY'S FAMILIAL DYNAMICS

First, I must describe a word we don't often use but which guides our understanding of Joseph's actions: *habitus*. The culture into which we are born influences how we respond to external forces. We are products of our culture, which, along with our family systems, shapes what we accept as true, real, and valuable. This includes social norms and morality—in essence, how one behaves within one's own culture. This becomes our *habitus*. This is true of Joseph as well. Understanding this helps us understand Joseph. I encourage you, dear reader, to recall what you already read in chapter 2 regarding the history that shaped Joseph's culture and keep this in mind as you read on.

Joseph faced challenges he never imagined—challenges that went beyond his cultural norms. His spiritual commitments conflicted with some cultural expectations, such as the stoning of an unfaithful woman. This was deeply troubling to him. Knowing the Old Testament law and the prescribed punishments, he found himself on the horns of a dilemma. Being faced with the weight of responsibility and being a just man, he began to survey his options. He must have debated within himself: "Do I exercise the law and

2. Calloway, *Consecration to St. Joseph*, 118.

allow her to be stoned? No, my love for her will not permit me to do that. Perhaps the best thing for me is to quietly divorce her?" It must have been a fitful night of sleep.

A FURTHER WORD ON HABITUS

How does a responsible man comport himself toward responsibility? Responsibility is a manifestation of integrity. The word *habitus* reminds us that Joseph was a product of the religious working class—his "tribe." How he spoke and acted reflected how he was formed. Integrity was part of who he was—it drove him. Integrity demands that actions match one's professed values. It is the quality of honesty, moral strength, and refusal to compromise. Responsibility is a willingness to be accountable for something within one's power. Integrity is the foundation from which responsibility flows.

When faced with difficult decisions, a mature and responsible person evaluates what actions are commensurate with his/her sense of morality. A choice must be made and translated into actions. "What happens before we have a chance to think about it is the source of what we call character."[3] Wilder continues, "When the master system has been disrupted . . . no character test is performed. People react according to their desires, feelings and emotions."[4] With Mary and Jesus, in everyday circumstances of wants and needs, Joseph's reactions reveal his character. Being the mature man he was, he responded as he knew his people would.

This habitus was what Jesus received from his culture and his earthly father. There are key words in the dreams that highlight Joseph's habitus: *responsible*, *just* or *righteous* (as some versions say), and *fear*. In the first dream, these words frame his response, showing his sense of duty, righteousness, and integrity.

---

3. Wilder, *Growing Me*, 42.
4. Wilder, *Growing Me*, 47.

ANGELS FROM THE REALMS OF GLORY

Joseph lived as his forebears had lived, and his understanding and behavioral response to the angel reflected his life pattern. His world conditioned him to respond well. As Matthew explains, "An angel of the Lord appeared to him in a dream" (Matt 1:20 ESV). God communicated to Joseph what his role was to be in the life of this child by sending an angel to deliver the message. The angel told him to stay in the marriage and name the child Jesus (meaning "God is salvation") to link him to the ancient promises and to the lineage of David, which connected Jesus to God's mission and promises. God's promise of redemption for mankind is a gathering of people from every tongue, tribe, and nation, reaching its fulfillment in the restoration of his creation.

It's easy to imagine Joseph was blindsided by a tsunami of emotions. The angel sought to calm his spirit and reassure him by saying "do not fear." We can relate to Joseph because we, too, can imagine how fear would grip us. Fear binds us; it can shut down reason and common sense and lead to inaction. The angel affirmed that Joseph was making the right, righteous decision and that he need not fear the outcome or future.

Matthew reports that Joseph awoke from his sleepy dream knowing "immediately" what to do and was ready to do it. (Character is what we do instinctively, before we think about it.) The immediate action Joseph took—responsibility—was normal to him. He was confident and willing to accept Mary and Jesus and participate in God's unfolding plan delivered to Abraham two thousand years earlier. It was natural for him to respond in cooperation with God's request.

"So, Joseph lived, as his forebears had lived, in a world saturated with angels. Because he was devout—because he was a just man—he followed the religious traditions of his ancestors. He attended the customary services. He said the prayers that he had been taught. And because of these habits, he was alert to the angels' presence and activity. He knew their company and their help."[5] No

---

5. Aquilina, *St. Joseph and His World*, 68.

Joseph Up Close and Personal

doubt he pondered all this and ruminated on this fulfillment of Isaiah's prophecy: "Behold the virgin shall conceive and bear a son, and they shall call his name Immanuel" (Matt 1:23 ESV). Though Joseph was consistently called "the carpenter," we might think of him as a "Mission Impossible" man. I like what author Mike Aquilina imagines: "He was always, it seems, in the midst of danger or high drama, or distant travel, or deep adventure. And those wild episodes were surely definitive for his life."[6]

Known as an ordinary workingman, "He would have commuted with other workers, to sites by walking, perhaps for miles. The worksites were noisy with the sound of hammers and saws and voices. Many of Joseph's co-workers were probably rough and uncouth."[7] Yet he was unique—one who was close to angels.

These angels were God's messengers. Knowing his Old Testament Scriptures, Joseph was well acquainted with angels. He was not surprised to encounter one four times, as Matthew reports it. Revering angels, he not only listened, but changed his plans according to God's message. Belief in angels was common in Joseph's time. Among the Jews, only the Sadducees denied their existence. The Scriptures abound with angelic appearances—from Genesis, Ezekiel, Daniel, Isaiah, to the New Testament Gospels, Acts, Epistles, and Revelation.

I don't believe Joseph feared for his life when the angel appeared. Rather, he might have feared failing in his responsibility. Raising Jesus to adulthood must have felt a Herculean, crushing task. As a young father, I remember feeling the weight of that responsibility deeply. It's easy to imagine all that could go wrong. The angel's message, "fear not," would have been a gentle, reassuring persuasion.

Mike Aquilina offers this idea: "The unspoken word of God's call is *trust*. Joseph was called to remember the marvels of the Lord—to remember the divine acts that were proclaimed in the synagogue and temple and at home—and trust the Lord who had

---

6. Aquilina, *St. Joseph and His World*, 69.
7. Aquilina, *St. Joseph and His World*, 70.

worked those marvels."[8] I can imagine Joseph sighing with relief upon receiving this reassurance.

NOT A FAMILY VACATION

Joseph's first dream is truly fascinating. Matthew tells us Herod sought to kill baby Jesus, viewing him as a threat to his throne. (Recall Herod was an Edomite, descended from Esau, who hated Jacob's descendants.) Old Testament prophecies, written over seven hundred years earlier, included this flight to Egypt: "Out of Egypt I called my son" (Hos 11:1). The hardships the holy family endured to get to Egypt, remain there, and return were epic. Though few records exist, cultural and historical context help us distinguish what is knowable and what is reasonable to believe.

Much information comes from the Coptic Orthodox Church. Some may be legendary, some factual. Thanks to John Mark, the Gospel writer who journeyed to Egypt after Pentecost, the Coptic Church was founded. From this community emerged scholars like Anthony of the Desert, Athanasius, and Clement of Alexandria. The Coptic Church has weathered many storms and remains strong.

POLITICS OF HIS ENVIRONMENT

Many factions existed in Judaism during Joseph's day. Scholars believe Joseph's family may have had ties to the Essenes, a sect eagerly awaiting the Messiah. They expected the Messiah would appear and lead the Essenes in league with heavenly armies of angels in a holy war against the Romans and all who would oppose the kingdom of God and the deliverance of the Jewish people.

The Dead Sea Scrolls contain the War Scroll describing this battle:

> But as for you, take courage and do not fear. . . . Israel is all that is and that will be. . . . Today is his appointed time to subdue and to humiliate the prince of the realm of

---

8. Aquilina, *St. Joseph and His World*, 77.

Joseph Up Close and Personal

wickedness. He will send eternal support to the company of his redeemed by the power of the majestic angel of the authority of Michael. By eternal light he shall joyfully light up the company of Israel—peace and blessing for the lot of God—to exalt the authority of Michael among the gods and the dominion of Israel among all flesh.[9]

Aquilina points out that "devotion to the angels was important to many of the Jewish authors whose works have survived from antiquity. It stood in continuity with the scriptures Joseph heard in the synagogue of Nazareth."[10]

THEIR FATHER-SON RELATIONSHIP

Joseph would have poured himself into Jesus. There is no doubt in my mind that Joseph kept closely attuned to the command of Deut 6:4–10:

> Hear, O Israel: The Lord our God, the Lord is one. You shall love the Lord your God with all your heart and with all your soul and with all your might. And these words that I command you today shall be on your heart. You shall teach them diligently to your children, and shall talk of them when you sit in your house, and when you walk by the way, and when you lie down, and when you rise. You shall bind them as a sign on your hand, and they shall be as frontlets between your eyes. You shall write them on the doorposts of your house and on your gates.

The intention of this command is that the parents are always in a teaching, forming mode, both formal and informal.

Joseph, being the fully mature man, would have carried this command to perfection with Jesus. I believe Joseph, knowing his Old Testament, would have had the understanding that his role with Jesus was to build a legacy around Jesus and Mary. It's easy and reasonable to see in Joseph many of the adjectives I'm bringing forward. In fact, for Joseph to build a legacy to last beyond

---

9. Aquilina, *St. Joseph and His World*, 67.
10. Aquilina, *St. Joseph and His World*, 67.

his own earthly presence, so that generations in the future might remember, rehearse orally, and transmit and record for future generations the life and love of Jesus for his creation, took great wisdom and determination. I posit that conclusion on the basis of my understanding of the biblical model of a legacy. For Joseph to fulfill the task God gave him, he had to accomplish the quality of life I've described in a legacy.

From where did Jesus get the training and understanding of the Passover Seder all Jews faithfully observed? Jesus grew up surrounded by a community of faithful Jews who, through their rituals, taught him. These were Joseph's and Jesus's people. Yet it was in the secure home of Joseph and Mary that Jesus learned the ritual, its meaning, and the proper protocol. Joseph taught him the ancient story of salvation. Joseph taught him how to bless the bread and break it, to bless the cup and share it. These family rituals were normal in the home of his father and mother. In short, the Shema in Deut 6:4 was both taught and caught as Jesus grew up. These formed an indispensable foundation for Jesus's public ministry—evidences of his inherited habitus.

ATTACHMENT AND BONDING

It was Jesus the boy's home life—with loving, devoted parents and upbringing—that produced Jesus the mature man who lived out his strong attachment to his heavenly Father. We'll explore this more in the following pages.

Attachment and bonding are two related child development concepts that interplay from birth. Bonding is what a new parent feels and does for their newborn. It starts when the child is born. It is emotionally connecting through relational activities, such as touch, close eye contact, synchronizing movements such as rocking, swaying, and mimicking facial expressions. These activities bring about changes in the brain's neurochemicals that allow for the parent to feel a closeness and warmth toward their child. From these positive emotions, the parent is enabled to meet their child's needs and ultimately aid in their positive development. This state of positivity may be better called a *state of joy*—a biblical concept of the mature person.

Attachment describes the enduring relationship that is created from the very moment the child is conceived and continues to be formed through the first few years of the child's life. When the child is attached to the parent, that child is given the message they are worthy to receive love and care and they can trust their caregiver to meet their needs. From the beginning, attachment is developing as the parent positively considers with anticipation the child's development in the womb and their coming birth. The needs that are met for the child in the womb, such as mother's nutrition, lifestyle habits, and overall mental, emotional, and physical health, are the beginning building blocks for attachment that will continue throughout their life. After birth, as the parent continues to meet the child's basic needs for survival—food, shelter, warmth, comfort—attachment from the child to the parent continues to grow.

Attachment and bonding develop continually throughout infancy and childhood in increasingly complex ways as the brain undergoes monumental growth stages. This process would have unfolded normally for Jesus, as he was raised in a loving and extended family, deeply connected to his people. He interacted with a multigenerational community of Yahweh worshippers.

THE DYNAMICS OF ATTACHMENT AND BONDING ILLUSTRATED

Luke 2 records an event when the holy family, as was their custom, attended the Passover Feast in Jerusalem. After the celebration, they had traveled a day's journey northward toward home before they realized Jesus was not with them. He had stayed behind in the city, worshipping and conversing with Jewish leaders. This caused panic and deep anguish for his parents—a nearly unbearable sorrow, a dark night of the soul. They searched for three days before finding him in the temple. Those three days must have felt interminably long, filled with tormenting "what ifs."

What Joseph and Mary felt was deep sorrow. Sorrow and pain arise whenever attachment is breached. Jesus, however, had already developed a strong, enduring attachment to his heavenly Father—something Joseph and Mary may not have fully understood. Mary was responding with the pain of a mother's attachment loss. Joseph, a just and silent man, was likely processing his anguish quietly and supportively. Perhaps neither had yet experienced the profound attachment Jesus displayed toward his heavenly Father.

Jesus was twelve years old—officially a man by Jewish custom—expected to account for himself socially, morally, and emotionally. He acted on what he had been taught so well that "all who heard him were amazed at his understanding and his answers" (Luke 2:47).

The dialogue that follows reveals a dynamic familiar to parents who have faced even temporary loss or absence of a child. Some words leap off the page in Luke 2:47–52: "They were astonished" to find him and that he understood what he was doing and the teachers' words. Mary said, as any good mother would, "Son, why have you treated us so?" This interchange illustrates attachment and bonding in action.

Mary continues: "Behold, your father and I" (a distinctly parental opening) "have been searching for you in great distress" (Luke 2:48). This expresses the anguish caused by attachment loss. It might be tempting to interpret this as a scolding, but it's really the pain of lost connection. Let me emphasize: when attachment is broken, the resulting pain is very real. Jesus's reply addresses that pain with the emotion of bonding. He quickly grasps Mary's motherly anguish and responds maturely: "Why were you looking for me? Did you not know that I had to be in my Father's house?" (Luke 2:49). The adults, however, did not understand what he meant.

Afterward, "he returned to Nazareth with them and was obedient to them" (Luke 2:51). Submission to his parents was an act of honor, as the law commanded, no matter his age. The precocious child had learned, "Honor your father and mother, that your days may be long in the land the Lord your God is giving you" (Exod 20:12 NLT). Submission means subordinating one's will and respecting another's wishes. Now of legal age, Jesus responded with maturity.

Here we see attachment and bonding interplay between the Son of God and his parents. Jesus, the twelve-year-old, submits to his parents after lovingly explaining he was doing what he learned from Joseph's life model. Reading between the lines, Jesus may have been saying he was at the temple because he was communing, as taught by his faithful community, with his heavenly Father. What Joseph taught, Joseph lived out in the community; Jesus did the same. Jesus's words carry two meanings simultaneously—he referred both to his earthly father and his heavenly Father. These meanings are mingled. This was part of his habitus. He caught it all. Jesus was fully attached and bonded to his heavenly Father as no human ever has been.

After Mary expressed her overwhelming fear for Jesus's life, she likely reflected on all the elements of the event: being unaware of his absence for three days, then finding him in the temple engaged in what was normal for his training—being about his Father's business. No doubt she opened her memory box and revisited the annunciation years before, described by Luke, remembering her response and lifelong dedication: "And Mary said, 'Behold, I am the servant of the Lord; let it be to me according to your word.'" (Luke 1:38 ESV). Mother Mary "treasured up all these things, pondering them in her heart" (Luke 2:19 ESV).

A final observation: Mary acted as the mother, Joseph like the strong, silent man he was. When they found Jesus, Mary did the talking. Joseph, as far as we know, spoke not a word. It fits his character that he was present, attentive to Mary's care as mother and Jesus as the object of their affection and protection. This was part of his ongoing responsibility. Luke, focusing on Jesus, did not emphasize Joseph. But he portrayed Joseph as supportive—always aware of and living his role well. Ordained by God as provider and caretaker, Joseph was responsible for the health and wellbeing of Mary and Jesus. After this event, Joseph is no longer mentioned. For certain, Jesus submitted to his earthly father. Their bond was demonstrated to the end!

JOSEPH'S ENDURING IMPACT

How does a man who was so silent, who never spoke a word that Scripture records, leave such a big imprint on the story of the birth of the God-man we know as Jesus, our Savior and Lord? Joseph was the one God appointed to be the agent to steward the earthly life of Jesus. A closer look at him will solidify our understanding of why God chose Joseph. It was because of Joseph's obedience and faithfulness to bond with his son that gave Jesus the possibility of attaching to Joseph and Mary. He grew up knowing they were close to him at all times, available to him in all situations and responsive to his needs.

Joseph still impacts us today, as a husband and father. His life is our inspiration to emulate him. As Pope Benedict XVI has written, "I wish to extend a particular word of encouragement to fathers so that they may take St. Joseph as their model. He who kept watch over the Son of Man is able to teach the deepest meaning of their own fatherhood."[11]

Joseph was that earthly father who availed himself of the rare privilege to attach to the Son of God. Joseph had an even more unique attachment than luminaries in the Old Testament, such as Abraham, Moses, and Isaiah and all the prophets. His attachment was physical, not a theophany or a voice, but in the flesh.

Joseph is, for us, the prototype of our salvific attachment to Jesus. When we identify with Christ through redemption, we are joined to him with a special bond. The apostle Paul in chapter 1 of Ephesians gives us a profound, enduring statement of what Christ has done for us:

> In love he predestined us for adoption to himself as sons through Jesus Christ. . . . In him we have redemption through his blood, the forgiveness of our trespasses . . . to unite all things in him, things in heaven and things on earth. . . . We have obtained an inheritance . . . sealed with the promise of the Holy Spirit. (Eph 1:4–11 ESV)

---

11. Quoted in Calloway, *Consecration to St. Joseph*, 32.

Joseph Up Close and Personal

Dallas Willard reminds us, "Salvation through a new, loving attachment to God that changes our identities would be a very relational way to understand our salvation: We would be both saved and transformed through attachment love from, to and with God."[12]

Thanks to St. Matthew's Gospel, we may see Joseph as a figure portrayed with the artistic technique called chiaroscuro—the treatment of light and shade to highlight a person or thing.[13] In Matthew's account, Joseph is highlighted as the strong, silent one. We sense his strength through the words and concepts Matthew uses. Let's look at some of those words illustrating this point.

THE GREAT ACTION: DREAM ONE, MATT 1:20

As we've already seen, angels were common to people in Joseph's day. We know that God is a self-revealing God. Psalm 8 gives us understanding how he reveals himself:

> Oh Lord, our Lord, how majestic is your name in all the earth! You have set your glory above the heavens. . . . When I look at your heavens, . . . the work of your fingers, the moon and stars, . . . what is man that you are mindful of him? . . . Yet you have made him a little lower than the heavenly beings [angels] and crowned him with glory, . . . given him dominion over the works of your hands; you have put all things under his feet. . . . O Lord, our Lord, how majestic is your name in all the earth! (ESV)

Joseph would have resonated deeply with these and other Old Testament Scriptures.

Joseph exercised good judgment in taking action as we've already noted. His action was to stay married to Mary, and to name the child Jesus. In dream number one, Matthew says Joseph was a "just man and unwilling to put her to shame, resolved to divorce her quietly" (Matt 1:19 ESV). The English Standard Version translation uses the word *just*, others use *righteous*. They have, largely,

---

12. Quoted in Wilder, *Renovated*, 6.

13. A good example of this is Caravaggio's painting *The Supper at Emmaus*, where exaggerated light reveals deep meaning.

the same meaning. They are common words in the Bible. "The privileged sense is that of moral rectitude, of imitation of God in his law multiple manifestations and in adherence to the law. Since this adherence is modeled on the relationship between two people, it varies with the changes in the relationship, but presupposes equity as indispensable."[14]

Joseph exercised good judgment. When he discovered Mary was pregnant, he resolved to divorce her quietly, because he was a "just man"—righteous, morally upright, and unwilling to shame her publicly (Matt 1:19 ESV). *Just* or *righteous* refers to moral rectitude, imitating God's law and fairness. Joseph was the kind of man who could always be counted on to do what was right. That is why, when the angel of the Lord commanded him, "he did as the angel of the Lord commanded him" (Matt 1:24).

THE GREAT ADVENTURE: DREAM TWO, MATT 2:13

After the Magi departed from Bethlehem, the angel appeared again: "Rise, take the child and his mother, and flee to Egypt, and remain there until I tell you, for Herod is about to search for the child, to destroy him" (Matt 2:13 ESV). The word *destroy* carries a chilling sense—more than murder, it implies annihilation, wiping out all memory of existence. Joseph's trust echoes Abraham's call from God: "Go from your country and your kindred and your father's house to the land I will show you—I will bless you and make your name great, so that you will be a blessing" (Gen 12:1–2 ESV). Joseph did exactly what God told him, with unwavering trust.

THE GREAT ANNOUNCEMENT: DREAM THREE, MATT 2:19-20

The angel then told Joseph: "Rise, take the child and his mother and go to the land of Israel, for those who sought the child's life are

---

14. Di Berardino, ed. *P–Z*, 414.

dead" (Matt 2:20 ESV). The waiting was over. Joseph must have breathed a sigh of relief, loaded the donkey, and headed home.

Here we see Joseph's obedience: doing what he's told, when he's told to do it, with the right heart attitude. Trust and obedience work hand in hand throughout these dreams.

THE GREAT ALERT: DREAM FOUR, MATT 2:21-22

Joseph obeyed and took action: "And he rose and took the child and his mother and went to the land of Israel" (Matt 2:21 ESV). Joseph was prepared to go but the alert would have raised a heightened sense of concern. I can imagine his trepidation to go at first; how would they establish and settle into a new home?

He would have also been nervous about the news that Archelaus was now ruling in Judea in place of his father, Herod, the despot. But, "he went and lived in a city called Nazareth, so that what was spoken by the prophets might be fulfilled, that he would be called a Nazarene" (Matt 2:23 ESV). I can't help but think his knowledge of the Old Testament was very affirming of the role God gave him. He would have been absolutely humbled to understand his place in the cosmic plan of God.

We should note, dreams three and four are similar. The difference is that in dream three the angel directs them back to Israel—the land of their birth. Dream four was to guide them to the exact place in the country to settle down. We might recall the star guiding the Magi to the country and city, then to the place where Jesus was.

THE ODYSSEY CONCLUDES

Here we close the story of Joseph and the most famous family ever—the story of heaven and earth joined in a married couple. To me, none could be greater. I cannot imagine, nor do I know of, any earthly marriage like theirs. They were unique—God made them so.

I wonder how many conversations Joseph and Mary had about their privilege to steward the Son of God's earthly life. How many times did they observe Jesus growing up, interacting with playmates, siblings, and extended family?

I could list countless questions I wish we had answers to. Yet speculation is only a game, as Scripture gives us only key facts and events, leaving much to ponder.

In the end, we take what we see—and what we don't see but still believe—about this man who stands alone in character: reliable, obedient, trusting, dependable, integral, faithful, tender, and loving toward God. Joseph is truly a man for all seasons. He is a model for all of us, but especially men, helping us grow in faith and emotional, spiritual, and social maturity. Neither Joseph nor Mary were perfect—but God chooses to work through imperfect people as we seek maturity in life.

DISCUSSION QUESTIONS AND PERSONAL REFLECTIONS: JOSEPH UP CLOSE AND PERSONAL

1. Our culture often defines masculinity in specific ways. Which of those traits do you see in Joseph? Which ones do you personally identify with, and why?

2. As you read the text, what stands out to you about Joseph's level of maturity? What clues are given that reveal his character and depth?

3. Let's talk about the concept of habitus—the ingrained habits, values, and behaviors shaped by our environment. How would you compare this to your understanding of a family system? In what ways are they similar or different?

4. Who were Joseph's people? Not in terms of tribal names, but the kind of individuals he would have identified with, trusted, and called his own. How do they shape how you see him?

5. From what we've learned so far, what did Joseph know about angels? How does that insight help you understand his

response to the angelic message about his planned marriage to Mary?

6. In Joseph's relationship with Jesus, what do you see that could encourage or inspire your own relationships—whether with your children, spouse, or others in your care?
7. In your everyday life, how do you approach emotional attachment and bonding? How might Joseph's example challenge or affirm your current priorities?
8. Revisit the story of Jesus in the temple from Luke 2. How does the idea of habitus help you see that event in a new light?

Chapter Four

Essentials for Maturity

Remember the days of long ago; think about the generations past. Ask your father, and he will inform you. Inquire of your elders, and they will tell you.

Deut 32:7 NLT

You have read the fuller story of Joseph—his background and the cultural context of his day. Now, it's time to consider where we go from here. I want to revisit what I introduced in chapter 3 about attachment, bonding, and relationships.

Let me be clear—I am not a psychologist. I share only what I've learned through six-plus decades of Christian service and now, as an elder desiring to pass on what I've gained. This project on Joseph is part of my effort to codify my own life. I see myself as a kind of kaleidoscope—turn the lens, and different insights appear. First came the importance of a well-conceived legacy, which exposed the immaturity I needed to conquer. Then came a deeper understanding of maturity's goal and a vibrant model—Joseph. I highly commend him to you.

ATTACHMENT

Brain science confirms attachment is indispensable in human relationships. Dr. James Wilder is a renowned, internationally known neurotheologian. His instructive words to us highlight the importance of attachment and love: "The only kind of love that helps the brain learn better character is attachment love. The brain functions that determine our character are most profoundly shaped by who we love."[1] This statement mirrors the Hebrew word *hesed*, variously translated as "devoted," "faithful," "loving-kindness," "unchanging," or "merciful" love. It is God's hesed love extended to us through redemption. Wilder, in quoting Dallas Willard, says, "Salvation through a new, loving attachment to God that changes our identities would be a very relational way to understand our salvation: We would both be saved and transformed through attachment love from, to, and with God."[2] Hosea captures this powerfully: "For I desire steadfast [hesed] love and not sacrifice, the knowledge of God rather than burnt offerings" (Hos 6:6 ESV).

ATTACHMENT TO GOD AND OTHERS

The Hebrew root for *attachment* means "cling," "adhere to," "follow," "join," or "stick with."[3] It applies both to human relationships and God's relationship with people. Consider:

- Human: "Then they lifted up their voices and wept again. And Orpah kissed her mother-in-law, but Ruth clung to her" (Ruth 1:14 ESV).
- Divine: "A man of many companions may come to ruin, but there is a friend who sticks closer than a brother" (Prov 18:24 ESV).

---

1. Wilder, *Renovated*, 6.
2. Wilder, *Renovated*, 6.
3. Wilder, *Renovated*, 113.

These verses affirm that God's love is shown in our willingness to remain attached in love to others. Wilder emphasizes that attachment is often the key to drawing people to God—whether they are losing faith or have never identified with Christ: "Feeling God is my enemy is not corrected by pointing out right beliefs about God. In such cases, a significant attachment to God's people often makes the difference."[4]

A PERSONAL NOTE ON ATTACHMENT

I have a close friend with whom I've met weekly for many years. He has spent over a decade studying what it means to be in relationship and truly attached to others. He is a man of impeccable integrity, with deep insight into biblical principles and the teachings of Jesus. I consider him a wise guide and coach. I've invited him into my life to help me grow in emotional and spiritual maturity.

You must understand the importance of attachment. Our salvation is, at its core, an attachment to Jesus—who sacrificially gave himself as a free gift to meet our deepest emotional and spiritual needs. Through this gift, we come to realize that we are worthy of love and can trust in a trustworthy provider. This is the foundation of attachment building. We are invited and drawn into his presence as beloved family members. We belong to our heavenly Father.

In the same way, we form attachment to friends and family when trust and mutual care have been built over time. My attachment to my friend reinforces this truth in both my mind and heart.

The ability to attach is fundamental to building relationships—and we do that to the level we are capable. Remember, it's a lifelong pursuit of increasing our capacity for attachment.

We learn by imitating those who model emotional and spiritual maturity, just as an infant learns to process emotions by witnessing and sensing their attached caregiver's expression of emotions.

This is attachment building. That's why the apostle Paul said to the Corinthians, "Be imitators of me, just as I also am of Christ" (1 Cor 11:1). Paul also wrote, ". . . until we all attain to the unity of

---

4. Wilder, *Renovated*, 123.

Essentials for Maturity

faith and of the knowledge of the Son of God, a mature man to the measure of the stature which belongs to the fullness of Christ. As a result, we are no longer to be children—but speaking the truth in love we are to grow up in all aspects into him" (Eph 4:13–15). This is the way God intended for us to live.

MORE ON ATTACHMENT

Another essential part of maturity is becoming spiritually complete. This requires an active, growing attachment *to* God. We are challenged to think *with* God, to become one of his people, and to spend time reflecting *on* him. Isaiah says, "Come now, and let us reason together says the Lord" (Isa 1:18 NLT). This is an invitation to think with God about our condition and our circumstances.

Dr. Wilder brings to our attention that *attachment is the strongest force in the human brain*. "The social brain is profoundly sculpted across the life span by who it loves. The quality of all relational interactions shapes the development of identity and character."[5] Jesus is the perfect example of this. He was fully human—complete. Luke 2:52 tells us that "Jesus grew in wisdom, stature, and favor with God and men." He had all the identity and relational skills needed to be human. Wilder writes, "Jesus completed his identity as a child. We have not completed ours; we must still work on it. Identity and relational skills are both learned. Holes in our identity must be filled for us to become mature." He goes on to say, "We do not know how to be human without learning from someone. The brain relies on attachment with those who have people skills to build and correct our identities. A good deal of practice must follow."[6] Relational skills can be built, much like muscle memory can be developed through practice. Maturity is built in relationship—with others and with God.

---

5. Wilder, *Renovated*, 50.
6. Wilder, *Renovated*, 154.

A PAUSE OF GREAT IMPORTANCE TO ME

To illustrate the importance of attachment in marriage, I must pause here to express my deep love and gratitude for my wife of sixty years. We were married June 25, 1965. We married young and we grew up together. When I speak about attachment and bonding, I cannot do so without acknowledging her profound influence on my character, my identity as a man, a husband, a father, and now a grandfather and great-grandfather. I cannot extol her virtues adequately. She knows me through and through. I count on her. I rely on her.

Proverbs captures what I feel about her: "Who can find a virtuous and capable wife? She is more precious than rubies. Her husband can trust her, and she will greatly enrich his life. She brings him good, not harm, all the days of her life. . . . She carefully watches everything in her household and suffers nothing from laziness. Her children stand and bless her. Her husband praises her: 'There are many virtuous and capable women in the world, but you surpass them all!'" (Prov 31:10–12, 27–29 NLT).

MATURITY AS A REASON FOR CHURCH MINISTRIES

Many churches today do not focus enough on helping men and women grow deeper in maturity. There will never be a fully mature man or woman this side of glory—only Jesus was fully mature. Still, the goal is for all of us to adopt and persevere in seeking wisdom, fixing the character flaws, and living a life of joy.

Wilder explains: "We can talk about things like spiritual maturity, but probably we should talk about spiritual *maturing*, which at some future point arrives at spiritual maturity."[7] Maturity is not a secret code, or a special gift reserved for a select group. Rather, "It's a matter of development that we can understand, devote ourselves to, and communicate to others."[8]

---

7. Wilder, *Renovated*, 55.
8. Wilder, *Renovated*, 14.

Essentials for Maturity

He continues: "Maturity refers to a process of growth. Immaturity stands at one end of the process, maturity at the other. And the growth process that results in maturity involves the essential components of the human being and some of the dynamics of their interaction."[9] To be a mature man is to be emotionally and spiritually whole. Since character governs our behavior, we must strive to be aware of our emotional state. Wilder writes, "The only way to have a rich emotional life is to not be dominated by emotions, but rather follow what is good with your emotions, your desires, and even your feelings."[10] As we grow deeper in character, we build the capacity to handle life with wisdom and stability, avoiding the trap of being ruled by fear, emotions, or feelings.

WHAT IS THE POINT?

I hope you've caught my passion for leaving a godly legacy—and my call for men to develop their own. Leaving a legacy requires men to grow deeper emotionally and spiritually.

Our culture is filled with men who are underdeveloped in maturity. This is not always their fault. Many did not grow up in loving, stable homes surrounded by godly people who could serve as "their people." All humans are immature to some degree. We all carry holes in our character. But few men ever learn how to recognize and overcome them. Men are called to monitor themselves, to identify their character that manifests in their behavior—and to work at closing those gaps.

To support this growth, I've pointed you to several helpful resources. In the bibliography, you'll find books that explain how the brain works, how character is formed, and how to assess and repair the gaps in your maturity.

A key step in this journey is learning how our early relationships shaped us—and how they affected each of the five stages of the brain's development.

---

9. Wilder, *Renovated*, 54.
10. Wilder, *Renovated*, 28.

THE HOLES IN OUR DEVELOPMENT

Attachment wounds are the holes formed when we didn't receive exactly what we needed during critical moments of development. From birth onward, our brains require specific relational input at every stage of growth. Ideally, parents meet these needs instinctively. But all those who recognize what they lacked growing up seek to do better for their own family.

To the degree those needs go unmet, we develop gaps, or holes, in our emotional and spiritual formation. These become barriers to healthy attachment and obstacles in building strong relationships.

I emphasize that our *attachment style* as adults is shaped by how consistently our needs were met in childhood. The book *Attachments: Why You Love, Feel, and Act the Way You Do* by Tim Clinton and Gary Sibcy explains this well. It describes attachment style as a *mental model*, a basic set of assumptions or core beliefs about yourself and others. These include the questions a person asks:

- About the self:
    - Am I worthy of being loved?
    - Am I competent to get the love I need?
- About others:
    - Are others reliable and trustworthy?
    - Are they accessible and willing to respond when I need them to be?[11]

These beliefs are not abstract—they are deeply ingrained through life experiences.

Today, science understands much more about the brain and how it develops. There are five major stages of brain development across the human lifespan: from birth, to childhood, to adulthood, parenting, and elderhood. Each stage has unique needs and developmental tasks. When a need goes unmet or a task is left incomplete, it creates a hole in that stage. If those holes aren't addressed,

---

11. Clinton and Sibcy, *Attachments*, 23.

Essentials for Maturity

they get carried into the next stage and compound. The result is immaturity that persists into adulthood.

These undeveloped areas do not resolve themselves over time. If we don't face them, we accumulate a lifetime catalog of unresolved issues. Many men take those issues to the grave—never confronting the parts of themselves they were too unprepared, or even lacking courage to face. When this happens, our legacy becomes distorted. It reflects not just what we accomplished, but also what we failed to confront. Our impact is diminished by what we were never courageous enough to change.

By the time a man reaches his senior years, he should be an elder. But many elders carry unresolved immaturities they've never confronted. A fully mature elder should be ready to champion community causes and share wisdom and love generously.

Remaining in immaturity limits the richness of life. An immature man settles for less—for himself and for his family—and misses the abundant life God desires for him. But when a man chooses to work on these holes, his life becomes filled with love, respect, and lasting treasure from family and friends. God's best is for all men to become elders by the time they enter their senior years.

SEEKING AND FILLING OUR HOLES

Here is a suggested palette of ideas to put you on the path toward maturity. These come from my own experiences—ways you might begin to deal with the holes in your life.

Please note: this is not a checklist, as if you're answering quiz questions and moving on once you've selected the "right" answer. Rather, it is a panoply of good things to consider, drawn from real life. You may be compelled to respond to different circumstances using different strategies at different times. Here are some suggestions for your personal development:

- Build a relationship with a godly, mature man—someone you can emulate and invite to speak into your life. Find a wise man to connect with—one with whom you can communicate freely, ask questions, seek advice, and process your thoughts. As Proverbs says: "Wisdom will multiply your days and add years to your life. If you become wise, you will be the one to benefit. If you scorn wisdom, you will be the one to suffer" (Prov 8:11–12 NLT).

- Recognize that many men are lonely, even if they have many acquaintances. Secular studies highlight this growing problem in our culture. The antidote is consistent, intentional time spent with other men. Deep relationships take effort and time—but they are worth it.

- Choose your friends carefully—especially the ones you are drawn to. They must be mature, godly men. These are the friendships you want to cultivate.

- Be willing to ask others what they see in you. Listen carefully to their wisdom. Watch how they respond to people and circumstances in their lives. "There are friends who destroy each other, but a real friend sticks closer than a brother" (Prov 18:24 NLT).

- Become a lifelong learner. Read quality books. Listen to helpful podcasts. Seek out resources that broaden your mind. Eleanor Roosevelt and many others have stated, "Great minds discuss ideas; average minds discuss events; small minds discuss people."

- Stay engaged with your culture, but don't let it define who you are.

- Study the work of Christians who are leaders in neurotheology and psychology—many are listed in the bibliography.

- Adopt a mindset that embraces who you want to become. Don't settle for who you've always been.

- Spend time with the Lord, asking him to help you become a spiritually mature and godly man. Seek his wisdom as you build your legacy. Remember, this is a lifelong journey—the Bible calls it sanctification.

- Keep your vision clear. Vision fades over time unless it's nurtured. The more you work on it, the more you build your capacity to shed immaturity. "Fear of the Lord is the foundation of true knowledge, but fools despise wisdom and discipline" (Prov 1:7 NLT).

- Practice, practice, practice. With consistent effort, you will begin to recognize and reshape old, immature patterns of behavior.

A PERSONAL COMMITMENT

I constantly face my own holes in development. I know how easy it is to live in poor habits that sabotage good intentions. Now that I'm a senior, I want to live and respond as an elder. I'm committed to growing and increasing my maturity. In fact, I'm committed to living an *elder life*, much like Paul instructed his own disciples.

I often reflect on Paul's advice to Titus, as he pastored and led the church in Crete: "As for you, Titus, promote the kind of living that reflects wholesome teaching. Teach the older men to exercise self-control, to be worthy of respect, and to live wisely. They must have sound faith and be filled with love and patience" (Titus 2:1–2 NLT).

REPRISE: LEGACY AND INTENTION

Let me repeat what I've already said about legacy: "These are the ingredients of a legacy—a life lived well; intentionally taught; subliminally caught; remembered and rehearsed orally; and transmitted and recast in writing for future generations."

A life lived well starts with the intention to leave a meaningful legacy. But to have a satisfying legacy, a man must grow in maturity—emotionally and spiritually. That growth must be intentional. It takes work.

WHERE DO WE GO FROM HERE?

The maturity challenge raises the question, "Where can I go to learn more about brain development, attachment, and why they matter for maturity?"

I encourage you to explore the works of Dr. Jim Wilder and others listed in the bibliography. Dr. Wilder is a leading psychologist and neurotheologian. Neuroscience has expanded rapidly in recent years, and Dr. Wilder has much to teach us. "He has lived, traveled, and taught in many cultures. He has observed the success and failure of customs, beliefs, and practices in communities that are rapidly disappearing. Jim developed this Life Model of maturity using many cultures, important developmental and spiritual teachings."[12]

Here are my recommendations for where to begin:

- *Living from the Heart Jesus Gave You* by James Friesen et al.
- *Maturity Pathway: A Companion Guide to "Living from the Heart Jesus Gave You" for Spiritual and Relational Growth* by Life Model Works.

These books provide a foundation for spiritual and relational growth. Then, move on to this trilogy:

- *Growing a More Human Community* by Jim Wilder

These explain the five stages of brain development in detail. I implore you—invest in your life by reading these books. You may experience breakthroughs in growth you never imagined. That is my prayer for you.

ONE MORE LOOK AT THE KEY WORDS OF MATURITY

Back in the introduction, I gave you a list of key words. These are not just helpful terms—they are words to ponder, evaluate, and integrate into your life. They will serve as guides when you face

---

12. Wilder, *Growing We the People*, back cover.

Essentials for Maturity

moments that require a mature response. All the words are important, but three in particular carry special weight. You'll find that becoming a mature man requires practicing all of them regularly. They are not a step-by-step sequence to "complete" but a set of tools you draw from as needed, depending on the moment.

- Consider *fear*

    Fear is hardwired into us from conception. Sometimes fear is helpful—for example, when we're in real danger. But fear also has a dark side. It often shows up when a situation exposes our immaturity. That's when we lash out in anger or rage, say things we regret, or behave in ways we know are wrong. "There is no fear in love. But perfect love drives out fear" (1 John 4:18).

- Think about *joy*

    Joy is also built into us from conception. God wants us to live in peace and learn to rest and quiet ourselves, to live in control of ourselves. When fear or anger rises, we can choose to step back and calm ourselves. The book *The Joy Switch* by Chris Coursey (listed in the bibliography) offers simple, practical exercises to help with this. I highly recommend it—it's an easy read with lasting impact.

- Now, hold on to your understanding of *attachment*

    Attachment is the space where joy is lived out in abundance. Enduring relationships grow from healthy attachment. We are attached to each other because we are first attached to Jesus: "God is love. Whoever lives in love lives in God, and God in them" (1 John 4:16). "Who then is the one who condemns? Christ Jesus is he who died, but rather, was raised, who is at the right hand of God, who also intercedes for us. Who shall separate us from the love of Christ? Shall tribulation, or distress, or persecution, or famine, or nakedness, or peril, or sword? . . . But, in all these things we overwhelmingly conquer through him who loved us" (Rom 8:34–35, 37).

Also, make it your goal to grow in emotional and spiritual maturity. Imitate those who are ahead of you on the path. Let their wisdom shape your own growth. These relationships are both the fruit of healthy attachment and the reward of maturity. They are your *tribe*.

Ultimately, all of these elements—fear, joy, attachment, maturity—make it possible to build a lasting, meaningful legacy.

Your legacy is made up of the people you've helped grow into maturity—those you've championed, encouraged, and taught to walk with God. This is the one gift you can carry with you to glory: the people you will see and dwell with in eternity.

My purpose in writing this book is to bring to your understanding how to live in joy and point you to tools that can help you, in the hope that you will become the man God created you to be. By taking this journey, you'll experience a profound paradigm shift—one for which, I believe, you will thank God every day.

DISCUSSION QUESTIONS AND PERSONAL REFLECTIONS: MATURITY

1. Why do you think love is so essential—not just to understand, but to actively live out? How does love shape your daily interactions with your family?

2. How would you describe your attachment to Jesus? In what ways does that relationship affect how you relate to others?

3. Do you have close friends you would describe as mature—people with whom you have strong emotional connection and trust? Why is that kind of bond important in your life?

4. When you compare maturity and immaturity, what differences stand out to you? How have you seen these traits impact real-life situations?

5. Why do you think immaturity can put a godly legacy at risk? Can you think of examples where this has been true?

Essentials for Maturity

6. What do you believe are the core ingredients of a lasting legacy? Why is it important to recognize and cultivate these as you shape your own?

In Conclusion

I suppose every author who agonizes over words for what feels like an interminable amount of time has a reasonable hope that people will read their work and gain insights to live a fruitful life. I am no less hopeful for you.

Now that you've read this book, you may sense there is more you want to learn. My desire is that you'll begin a plan to actively follow your heart. Life unfolds in chapters, and each new season presents opportunities to continue maturing and gaining wisdom. These chapters often become the very challenges God uses to grow us—if we choose to cooperate with him.

My own story illustrates this truth. I often say my life has two parts: the first, from birth to the death of my firstborn son; and the second, everything since. I grew up in a Christian home with parents who, despite good intentions, didn't know how to guide me through the developmental needs of my early years. When I married, I was still carrying unaddressed immaturity (not that I would've recognized it—honestly, I might have been insulted to be told).

When my son was murdered in 1992, my second half of life began. That event literally changed me. I had been impulsive, aggressive, determined to succeed, task oriented, selfish. I was hard-charging and hell-bent on proving I had worth. These traits of immaturity existed because I grew up in a family system where much of what I needed wasn't provided. In that first half of life,

I had learned how to manage my immaturity—how to hide it, at least from myself.

But after the loss of my son, everything changed. My wife and our other two children began a journey of living out the reality of forgiveness. Since that day—and until the day I die—I will never be the same. God has tenderized me. He has made me more loving, more compassionate, and more caring.

Life is full of choices. We can't control many of our circumstances, but we *can* choose how we respond—and what we will do about our state of immaturity. I chose to believe that God was still in control and that I could trust him at all times. For the past thirty-three years, God has consistently affirmed his love (hesed) for me. He has given me countless opportunities to use my story, both to sharpen myself and to serve as a catalyst in the personal growth of others.

I've come to believe that building a legacy is not just valuable—it's necessary. That's true for me, and I believe it's true for all men. In our culture, I've observed that many men have lost their way. There's deep confusion—even within the church—about what it means to be a mature man. We see this crisis in public life and in spiritual leadership. Sadly, we are in short supply of mature statesmen—men who embody the qualities we need and whom we can trust to lead.

This book is an invitation. A call to renew our efforts to challenge men to take responsibility for their growth—and to support them as they rise to the challenge.

I've attempted to define the problem of immaturity and contrast it with true maturity. I've focused on the example of Joseph as someone who was committed to living this out, shown the results a godly legacy can bring, and pointed toward resources where more help can be found. And yes—I'm still working on my own immaturity. The truth is, none of us will ever arrive at perfect maturity. We're called to keep growing. Always. You'll find recommendations for further help in the bibliography. I urge you: take this seriously.

Appendix A

Two Josephs

*The Old Testament Patriarch
and the New Testament St. Joseph*

As Almighty God appointed Joseph, son of the patriarch Jacob, over all the land of Egypt to save the grain for the people, so when the fullness of time was come and he was about to send to earth his only-begotten Son, the Savior of the world, he chose another Joseph of whom the first had been another type, and he made him the lord and chief of his household and possessions, the guardian of his choicest treasures.[1]

POPE PIUS IX

THERE ARE PROFOUND TRUTHS we can glean about St. Joseph by reflecting on the Old Testament Joseph—the one with the coat of many colors, who was sold into slavery by his jealous brothers and eventually rose to power in Egypt, becoming second only to the Pharaoh. Let us wade into the truths revealed in the life of the Old Testament Joseph, which sheds light on new dimensions to our understanding of St. Joseph.

---

1. Quoted in Calloway, *Consecration to St. Joseph*, 77.

Appendix A

"If God normally prefers to use creatures as his instruments for communicating truth, grace, and salvation, it is reasonable to think that God uses certain saints as privileged instruments to bring about a closer union with him."[2]

In theological terms, this is called *typology*. A type is a foreshadowing—a person or object that anticipates and points toward a later, fuller reality. Types guide us from knowledge of one person or event (such as the serpent in the wilderness or, in this case, the patriarch Joseph) to greater knowledge of the person or reality they prefigure. Typology helps us understand divine revelation on a larger scale.

This is grounded in the truth of our salvific relationship to God through Christ. Because we are attached to him, we are drawn into attachment relationships with one another. Jesus affirmed this when he prayed "that they may all be one, just as you, Father, are in me, and I in you, that they also may be in us, so that the world may believe that you have sent me" (John 17:21 ESV).

We are in relationship with both Josephs as spiritual kin. They are part of that great cloud of witnesses, where we too will be, along with all who die in Christ, according to Heb 12:1.

WHAT MAKES A TYPE?

We must be careful not to assume too quickly that someone or something is a type. There are criteria for determining this. "A likeness is clear when there are multiple and distinct parallels between the type and its fulfillment. A likeness is distinct when it is uncommon and unique."[3] In other words, we must identify clear and specific parallels in order to recognize one figure as a type and the other as its fulfillment. "The ability of a type to call to mind that of which it is a type is the key element which gives force and power to arguments by way of typology."[4] It benefits us to thoughtfully

---

2. Walshe, *Saint Joseph*, 7.
3. Walshe, *Saint Joseph*, 13.
4. Walshe, *Saint Joseph*, 14.

Two Josephs

examine such reasons, because they hold spiritual value and can help shape the way we live.

I borrow three principles from author Sebastian Walshe that clarify how to interpret the Old and New Testaments accurately:

1. "Be especially attentive to the content and unity of the whole of Scripture.
2. Read Scripture within the living tradition of the Church.
3. Be attentive to the analogy of faith—that is, to the coherence of the truths of faith among themselves."[5]

There is an old saying, often attributed to St. Augustine, that my pastor taught me as a teenager: "The New is concealed in the Old, and the Old is in the New revealed."

By recognizing types, we are reminded of God's omniscience and his unfailing promises as revealed through the lives of those who came before us.

SIX PARALLELS BETWEEN THE TWO JOSEPHS

Sebastian Walshe identifies six ways the Old Testament patriarch Joseph foreshadows St. Joseph, the husband of Mary. The concepts are:

1. Both share the same name.
2. Both have fathers named Jacob. Matthew 1:16 identifies St. Joseph's father as Jacob—the only other Joseph in Scripture with a father of the same name, which is unique.
3. God speaks to both through dreams (Gen 37:5; Matt 1:20).
4. Both are forced to journey to Egypt (Gen 37:28; Matt 2:14).
5. Both refused to have relations with a woman they should not have, Joseph the patriarch with Potiphar's wife and St. Joseph with Mary (Gen 39:7–9; Matt 1:25).
6. Both are appointed rulers over the household and possessions of a king. The patriarch Joseph ruled all of Egypt (Gen

---

5. Walshe, *Saint Joseph*, 23.

Appendix A

41:40–44). St. Joseph was the head of the holy family, guardian of God's greatest treasures—Jesus and Mary (Luke 2:51).[6]

To circle back, Pope Leo XIII (reigned 1878–1903) articulated St. Joseph's role clearly: "St. Joseph, in virtue of his relationship to Mary and Jesus, had the responsibility to care for the Holy Family: 'From this two-fold dignity flowed the obligation which nature lays upon the head of families, so that Joseph became the guardian, the administrator, and the legal defender of the divine house whose chief he was. And during the whole course of his life, he fulfilled those charges and those duties.'"[7]

It seems evident, then, that the patriarch Joseph was a type of the greater fulfillment found in St. Joseph. Because St. Joseph faithfully fulfilled his divine mission, he helped secure the success of the Messiah and the establishment of God's people. In response, we as the church affirm this legacy each week when we proclaim the Apostles' Creed:

> I believe in God the Father, who created heaven and earth; and in Jesus Christ, God's only Son, our Lord, who was conceived by the Holy Spirit, born of the Virgin Mary, was crucified, died and buried.
>
> He descended into hell; the third day he rose from the dead, he ascended into heaven and sits at the right hand of God, the Father Almighty. From thence he will come to judge the living and the dead. I believe in the Holy Spirit, the Holy Catholic Church, the communion of Saints, the forgiveness of sins, the resurrection of the body, and life everlasting. Amen.[8]

---

6. Walshe, *Saint Joseph*, 30.
7. Quoted in Walshe, *Saint Joseph*, 47.
8. Apostles' Creed, *United Methodist Hymnal*, 881.

Two Josephs

A CONCLUDING THOUGHT ON JOSEPH THE PATRIARCH

Typology also points us toward a larger theological idea: progressive revelation. This concept means that God's truth and plan for humanity were gradually revealed over time. As though unrolling a long scroll, foundational truths appear early and give way to deeper insight. The more one reads, the more clearly one sees the fullness of God's purpose.

This understanding was present in the church as early as the second century. "One of its most vocal proponents was Irenaeus of Lyons, a disciple of John the Apostle. He affirmed the absolute unity of God, while also recognizing that the new covenant had fulfilled and surpassed the old. This, he argued, showed that God was leading humankind gradually toward final perfection."[9]

Jesus affirmed this unfolding when, on the road to Emmaus, he explained the Scriptures to two travelers: "And beginning with Moses and all the prophets, he explained the things concerning himself in all the Scriptures. . . . And their eyes were opened and they recognized him" (Luke 24:27, 31 RSV).

Jesus also said, "The Son of Man did not come to be served, but to serve, and to give his life as a ransom for many" (Matt 20:28). In the patriarch Joseph, we see a type—a foreshadowing—of a greater truth to come. Through progressive revelation, God helps us interpret the Bible as a unified story. From Genesis we receive the initial promise of God's plan for mankind—then he chose Joseph to save the Hebrew people. As the New Testament teaches, he chose St. Joseph and Mary to fulfill his covenant promise to Abraham, that through his descendants, all nations would be blessed by the coming of the Messiah, slain from the foundation of the world as we read in Rev 13:8.

As we reflect on both Josephs, we are invited to marvel at how God's promises and patterns have unfolded throughout salvation history.

---

9. Di Berardino, *P–Z*, 316–17.

Appendix B

If—

BECAUSE I AM A man, a father, a husband, a grandfather, and a great-grandfather—as well as an elder in my community—one who strives to build a godly legacy and leave the sweet aroma of Jesus Christ for those who come after me, Rudyard Kipling's poem "If—" speaks deeply to my heart. I am grateful for the swirling entourage around me, to whom I give my loyalty and, as best I can, everything I have gained over my lifetime. I pray they will find my memories sufficient to draw courage and build their own legacy. This is the essence of passing the faith along: "So each generation should set its hope anew on God" (Ps 78:7a NLT).

IF—

> If you can keep your head when all about you
> Are losing theirs and blaming it on you;
> If you can trust yourself when all men doubt you,
> But make allowance for their doubting too;
>
> If you can wait and not be tired by waiting,
> Or, being lied about, don't deal in lies,
> Or, being hated, don't give way to hating,
> And yet don't look too good, nor talk too wise;

If—

If you can dream—and not make dreams your master;
If you can think—and not make thoughts your aim;
If you can meet with triumph and disaster
And treat those two impostors just the same;

If you can bear to hear the truth you've spoken
Twisted by knaves to make a trap for fools,
Or watch the things you gave your life to broken,
And stoop and build 'em up with worn-out tools;

If you can make one heap of all your winnings
And risk it on one turn of pitch-and-toss,
And lose, and start again at your beginnings
And never breathe a word about your loss;

If you can force your heart and nerve and sinew
To serve your turn long after they are gone,
And so hold on when there is nothing in you
Except the Will which says to them: "Hold on";

If you can talk with crowds and keep your virtue,
Or walk with kings—nor lose the common touch;
If neither foes nor loving friends can hurt you;
If all men count with you, but none too much;

If you can fill the unforgiving minute
With sixty seconds' worth of distance run—
Yours is the Earth and everything that's in it,
And—which is more—*you'll be a Man, my son*!

Rudyard Kipling (1865–1936)

Appendix C
A Biblical Definition of Love

I CANNOT, AND MUST not, conclude this project without highlighting the great definition of love given in the immortal, inimitable words of 1 Corinthians 13. All the themes of legacy, maturity, relationships, attachment, and bonding rest upon this foundational truth—*love*. Read these words slowly and contemplate the depth of human relationships they reveal.

> If I could speak all the languages of earth and of angels, but didn't love others, I would only be a noisy gong or a clanging cymbal. If I had the gift of prophecy, and if I understood all of God's secret plans and possessed all knowledge, and if I had such faith as could move mountains, but didn't love others I would be nothing. If I gave everything I have to the poor and even sacrificed my body, I could boast about it; but if I didn't love others, I would have gained nothing. Love is patient and kind. Love is not jealous or boastful or proud or rude. It does not demand its own way. It is not irritable, and it keeps no record of being wronged. It does not rejoice in injustice but rejoices whenever the truth wins out. Love never gives up, never loses faith, is always hopeful, and endures through every circumstance. Prophecy and speaking in unknown languages and special knowledge will become useless, but love will last forever! Now our knowledge is partial and incomplete, and even the gift of prophecy

A Biblical Definition of Love

reveals only part of the whole picture! But when the time of perfection comes, these partial things will become useless. When I was a child, I spoke and thought and reasoned as a child. But when I grew up, I put away childish things. Now we see imperfectly, like puzzling reflections in a mirror, but then we will see everything completely, just as God now knows me completely. Three things will last forever—faith, hope and love—and the greatest of these is love. (1 Cor 13 NLT)

Appendix D

The Legacy of the Apostles

THE PRIMARY LEGACY THE apostles left was relational. Through life-on-life contact the apostles invested in, taught, and discipled and mentored others, multiplying the harvest and expanding the church. They were followed in the first century of Christianity by others whom the Lord had touched. Those who believed their message carried on the work of reaching the world. We have the privilege of standing on the shoulders of the millions who followed in the wake of the legacy left by the apostles.

Jesus gave these twelve courageous men a clear mandate recorded in Matt 28:19–20: to take his message to all the world. Their journeys were remarkable. It's fascinating to trace their steps, according to church tradition.

- Thomas went to Syria, Iran, and India.
- James the son of Zebedee was beheaded in Jerusalem. James preached to the one who guarded him. The guard was convicted of the righteousness of Jesus. Declaring his newfound faith he knelt and accepted beheading as a Christian.
- Andrew went to Russia and also preached in Turkey and Greece.
- John went to Ephesus, ultimately exiled on the isle of Patmos.
- Matthew went to Persia and Ethiopia.

The Legacy of the Apostles

- Phillip went to North Africa and Asia Minor.
- Nathanael went to India, Armenia, to Ethiopia and southern Arabia.
- James the son of Alpheus went to Syria.
- Simon the Zealot went to Persia.
- Matthias went to Syria with Andrew.
- James, leader of the Jerusalem church, ultimately was thrown to his death off the pinnacle of the temple.

There are, no doubt, thousands of such examples, far too numerous in this space to tell. We can certainly appreciate the *legacy* they left; their impact on the world of humanity is remarkable.

About the Artist Eva Crawford

Eva Crawford is an award-winning artist with a BFA from UNC–Chapel Hill and a lifetime of art making. Her interactions with former high school students and her own five children, including a son from Uganda, taught Crawford to make art about human stories. Additionally, her exposure to those navigating mental illness compels her to pay attention to others' feelings and their need to be understood. Therefore, Crawford's art is largely portraiture.

Crawford's portraits are grounded in relationships with those we love, with those for whom we feel compassion, and with those whom we do not yet understand. Crawford addresses healing through paintings and drawings of people by investigating the unity of the human experience. Her work ranges from expressive to intricately slow artworks that reflect the necessary time required to know another human and to gain deeper understanding. Crawford's materials include watercolor, acrylic, charcoal, and collage, and range in size from notecard to wall mural. Just as personalities vary, so do her art investigations.

Crawford is well established in her career, yet she welcomes the daily challenge of staying true to her unique artistic voice and creating work that responds to that voice.

In the creating and marketing of her art, it is her desire that God be glorified and honored (Col 3:17).

Contact Eva Crawford:

Appendix D

Eva Crawford
118 E. Kingston Ave., Studio 22,
Charlotte, NC 28203
E-Mail: evacrawfordart@gmail.com

Bibliography

Apostles' Creed. In *The United Methodist Hymnal*, 881. Nashville: United Methodist, 1989.

Aquilina, Mike. *St. Joseph and His World*. New York: Scepter, 2020.

Calloway, Donald H. *Consecration to St. Joseph: The Wonders of Our Spiritual Father*. Stockbridge, MA: Marian Fathers of the Immaculate Conception of the B.V.M., 2020.

Clinton, Tim, and Gary Sibcy. *Attachments: Why You Love, Feel, and Act the Way You Do*. Nashville: Nelson, 2009.

Coursey, Chris M. *The Joy Switch: How Your Brain's Secret Circuit Affects Your Relationships—And How You Can Activate It*. Chicago: Northfield, 2021.

Di Berardino, Angelo, ed. *P–Z*. Vol. 3 of *Encyclopedia of Ancient Christianity*. Translated by Erik A. Koenke et al. Downers Grove, IL: IVP Academic, 2014.

Friesen, James G., et al. *Living from the Heart Jesus Gave You*. Peoria, IL: Shepherd's House, 2024.

Graham, Billy. "Billy Graham: The Greatest Legacy." Billy Graham Library, February 4, 2024. https://billygrahamlibrary.org/blog-billy-graham-the-greatest-legacy/.

Guzman, Sam. *The Catholic Gentleman: Living Authentic Manhood Today*. San Francisco: Ignatius, 2019.

Kipling, Rudyard. "If—." Poetry Foundation. https://www.poetryfoundation.org/poems/46473/if---.

Lerner, Alan Jay, and Frederick Loewe. *Camelot: A Musical*. New York: Random House, 1961.

Life Model Works. *Maturity Pathway: A Companion Guide to "Living from the Heart Jesus Gave You" for Spiritual and Relational Growth*. Peoria, IL: Shepherd's House Inc., 2024.

Mohr, Jon. "Find Us Faithful." Track 5 on *People Need the Lord*, performed by Steve Green, produced by Greg Nelson. Sparrow Records, 1988.

Patrignani, Anthony J. *A Manual of Practical Devotion to St. Joseph*. Rockford, IL: TAN, 1982.

Bibliography

Peterson, Eugene H. *A Long Obedience in the Same Direction: Discipleship in an Instant Society.* Lisle, IL: InterVarsity, 1980.

Priestap, Jean. "It Started with a Sunday School Teacher!" Vision for Christ, March 8, 2017. https://visionforchristworld.com/it-started-with-a-sunday-school-teacher/.

Walshe, Sebastian. *Saint Joseph: The Man Closest to Christ.* Gastonia, NC: TAN, 2023.

Wilder, Jim. *Growing Me: Becoming a Child.* Vol. 1 of *Growing a More Human Community.* Rev. ed. Evergreen, CO: Fast Track, 2024.

———. *Growing Us: Becoming an Adult.* Vol. 2 of *Growing a More Human Community.* Rev. ed. Evergreen, CO: Fast Track, 2024.

———. *Growing We the People.* Vol. 3 of *Growing a More Human Community.* Rev. ed. Evergreen, CO: Fast Track, 2024.

———. *Renovated: God, Dallas Willard, & the Church That Transforms.* Colorado Springs: NavPress, 2020.

Wilder, Jim, and Michel Hendricks. *The Other Half of Church: Christian Community, Brain Science, and Overcoming Spiritual Stagnation.* Chicago: Moody, 2020.

www.ingramcontent.com/pod-product-compliance
Lightning Source LLC
Chambersburg PA
CBHW071739090426
42738CB00011B/2530